People who Shaped China

Book One

Stories from the history of
the Middle Kingdom

Preface

Over 2,000 years ago, the First Emperor united China under the Qin Dynasty, which is where we get the name "China." After the Qin was the golden age of the Han Dynasty. Even today, the Chinese call themselves the Han people, their speech the Han language, and their writing Han characters.

There have been dozens of Chinese dynasties and hundreds of emperors. Different parts of the country have different customs and dialects, but they all share the same history, learning from the great men and women who shaped China and its 5,000 years of civilization.

Foreword

When President Donald Trump visited Beijing, he showed a video of his granddaughter Arabella Kushner speaking Mandarin to the Chinese leader. The two-minute clip went viral on the internet, and Arabella became a minor celebrity among Chinese viewers.

Like Ms. Kushner, more and more people are learning Chinese as China re-emerges as a great power with global influence. Yet for the majority of westerners, China remains a very foreign country, and the Chinese a perplexing people.

Seen from a historical vantage point, China is a very unique nation. It has been said that American history is divided into decades, European history into centuries, and Chinese history into millennia. For the last 3,000 years, China is the only country in the world that has kept unbroken historical records. People and events of the distant past fill the memories of the Chinese people. It was they who created Chinese civilization and culture, and the people living in China today.

Isolated from the rest of the world, millions of square miles of land within great natural barriers gave rise to a unique civilization. To the east and south is the endless Pacific Ocean. In the north, steppes and deserts stretch into the frozen Siberian tundra. In the west lies the plateau of Tibet and the massive peaks of the Himalaya mountains.

Two great rivers, the Yellow River and Yangtze Jiang, flow ceaselessly from west to east. The people living there called their nation the Central Country—China.

History is abstract, but its characters were real, living people. Each civilization is rooted in its history. The history remembered by its people guides its journey into the future. To understand the Chinese, we must understand Chinese culture. To understand Chinese culture, we must understand Chinese history.

Presented in three volumes are stories of characters who shaped the history of the Chinese from past to present. By knowing them, you will begin to understand today's China.

Project Manager: Xiao Liao

Writing and Editing: Xiao Liao and Leo Timm

Translation: Leo Timm and Eva Fu

Translation Assistance: Yuyam Liao, Qiqi Wang and Beiyao Wang

Proofreading: Steven Wu and Su Lin

Illustration: Mingguo Sun and Chenchen Sng

Layout: Mingguo Sun

Cover Design: R One

Special thanks to: Jingwen Wang and Bailey Li

© 2018 New Epoch International USA
People Who Shaped China, Book One

Table of Contents

0
Pan Gu
Creation of the universe

Like all other ancient cultures, as Chinese civilization grew, it sought to explain the beginnings of the universe and the origin of existence.

Before the creation of the universe, the cosmos was an enormous empty egg. There was no north or south, no east or west. It contained nothing but void matter and a sleeping giant named Pan Gu.

Finally, Pan Gu awoke from his eons of slumber. He was surrounded by stuffy blackness and could hardly move. Irritated, he split open the cosmic shell.

From the egg exploded layers and layers of existence, from the most microscopic energy particles to stars and galaxies. Light and clarity ascended to become the endless heavens, while heavy murkiness sank to form the vast earth.

Pan Gu looked around with wonder. Fearing that the heavens and the earth would become one again, he decided to do something about the unbearable confines that had trapped him for so many years. For another epoch lasting 18,000 years, Pan Gu stood like a pillar between heaven and earth, separating them forever.

Finally, Pan Gu had no more strength. As Pan Gu lay dying, his body transformed. His left eye became a scorching red sun and his right eye, a cool silver moon. His last gasp of breath became the invisible wind and the cloaking white clouds. His final voice became the thunder.

His hair and beard transformed into the stars and the Milky Way. His limbs became mountains standing in the four universal directions. The blood running through his veins transformed into rivers, his tendons paved into roads, and his muscles disintegrated into fertile lands. His skin and sweat pores blossomed into flowers, trees, and plants; his teeth and bones shaped into metals, precious stones, jades, and splendid treasures. His sweat fell as raindrops on the earth that had now come into being.

According to this ancient Chinese legend, spirit and substance came into existence at the same time. There was the egg, and with it came Pan Gu's will to crack it open and release all life from within.

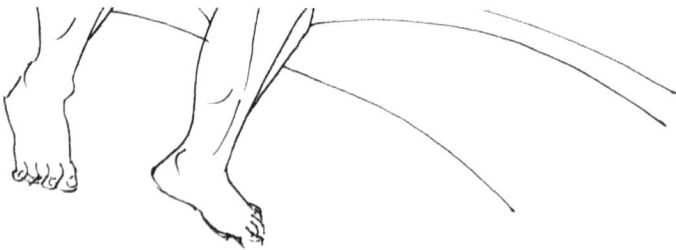

Nü Wa
Birth of mankind

All great civilizations have stories about how gods created man. For thousands of years, the Chinese people have passed down the legend of Nü Wa, the goddess who crafted people from clay.

When the world was still new and empty, Nü Wa descended to the earth and strode along the Yellow River. She peered into the water and marveled at her own beautiful reflection, but she felt lonely. Reaching into the river, she picked up a handful of yellow clay and molded a small miniature figure of herself. She then took two glistening black pebbles from the water, and turned them into her figure's eyes. Nü Wa set her figure on the ground, and it came to life and called her "mama."

Delighted, Nü Wa happily kneaded and molded more and more people from the yellow clay, with their eyes crafted from the glistening black pebbles. Yet as she kneaded, her fingers blistered, and she realized how few of her children there were to cover the vast land.

She dipped a reed stalk into the wet clay of the river and flung it in the air, sending droplets flying all around. Wherever a drop hit the ground, life was created, and out sprouted a human being. Nü Wa traveled the land, dipping her stalk into the clay and creating men and women to fill the beautiful empty world with life.

Nü Wa loved and protected her children. With heavenly tools, she and her husband, Fu Xi, set the laws of nature and

put the
universe in
order. Day and night and
the two forces of yin and yang were
formed.

The humanity that Nü Wa created prospered. However, she would soon have to save them.

The God of Water rebelled against heaven, and the heavens sent the God of Fire to conquer him. The God of Water was defeated, but he fell to earth and crushed Mount Buzhou, a mountain pillar propping up the heavens. The sky cracked, and the earth broke. Nü Wa could only watch as her people were drowned and burned.

Nü Wa was desperate. She searched everywhere for all the precious stones and metals she could find and melted them into a sacred boulder of five brilliant hues.

Despite the scalding heat, Goddess Nü Wa hauled the molten boulder and flew toward the huge hole in the sky to mend it. She held it there until the boulder cooled and the floods stopped. The people Nü Wa had created survived to play out the 5,000 years of Chinese history.

1
The Yellow Emperor
Civilization begins

According to Chinese legends, civilization began when gods taught their secrets to mankind. Sui Ren taught man how to use fire to cook. You Chao showed man how to build houses and forts for protection against storms and beasts. The Dragon Master Fu Xi passed on the knowledge of yin and yang and created the rites of marriage between husband and wife.

As people learned the ways of the gods, their numbers increased. Shen Nong, the Divine Farmer, studied hundreds of plants and herbs and discovered their nutritional and medical values. Mankind invented agriculture, and civilization was born.

One of Shen Nong's descendants was named Yan. His tribe resided in the Yellow River Valley, a fertile land where the early Chinese grew their crops. Because of Shen Nong's famous deeds, this tribe became the most respected in the region.

Another large tribe, the Nine Li, lived to the south. They were a powerful and war-oriented race. They were friendly with Yan's people, but that changed when Chi You took over as their leader.

Chi You led the Nine Li to attack and seize land belonging to Yan. Chi You had many brothers, and it was said that all of them had heads and arms made of bronze, making them immune to the blows of swords and spears. Yan's farming folk were no match for them.

It was then that the Yellow Emperor, Huang Di, appeared. He and his tribe accepted the Yan refugees as their own people, but Chi You was offended and sent his army to attack the Yellow Emperor.

The Nine Li were deadly soldiers, skilled not just in direct combat but also in their use of fire and smoke on the battlefield. They even had the power to command mighty floods. The Yellow Emperor's men faced water and flames whichever way they went, and they lost 71 battles. But the Yellow Emperor had the gods on his side.

Heaven gave uniforms to the Yellow Emperor's army and books to the Yellow Emperor to teach him to organize his soldiers for battle. He invented a war chariot that could quickly transport troops anywhere they were needed, and drums to give commands to his soldiers at long range. A tribe that lived on the steppe pledged loyalty to the Yellow Emperor and provided tamed horses to support his army. He also prayed to the gods of wind and drought to come to his aid.

In the final battle with Chi You, the Yellow Emperor's tribe crushed the Nine Li. Chi You was killed, and his followers escaped to the south. They became the Miao and other ethnic minorities living in southern China and Southeast Asia, and some worship Chi You to this day.

The Yellow Emperor's people formed the earliest Chinese society. Modern Chinese people regard themselves as the descendants of the Yellow Emperor and the Yan tribe.

The emperor's wife, Lei Zu, discovered how to make silk from the cocoons of worms and passed this art among the tribes. As a result, silk was a special symbol of China for thousands of years.

Cang Jie, one of the Yellow Emperor's officials, gathered the footprints of birds and beasts and used them to create writing—the first Chinese characters.

At the end of his rule, the Yellow Emperor held a ceremony to offer his respects to the gods. Legend has it that as the incense burned, a yellow dragon came down from the sky, carried the Yellow Emperor on its back, and ascended with him to heaven.

Emperor Yao
Ruled With Selflessness and Virtue

"If there is but a single man who goes hungry, it is I who am responsible."

A famous Chinese myth tells of how in the ancient days, there were ten suns in the heavens. Every day they took turns riding their divine chariots out across the sky, warming the earth below them.

One day, the suns decided to come out all at once. People shriveled and perished as the water in the rivers dried up, the trees in the forests turned to ashes, and the earth burned.

Emperor Yao dispatched his most talented warrior, a godlike archer, to shoot down the suns. But the demon suns escaped unscathed.

Desperate, the emperor consulted his wisest minister. The minister

gave the following advice: "Hou Yi may have his divine arrows, but the matter rests with the piety of the sovereign."

Upon hearing these words, Emperor Yao made a trip to Mount Kunlun, the mountain where Heaven touches Earth. He bathed himself in the mountain streams. He abstained from wine and meat. He prayed to the gods and his ancestors.

Sure enough, good news reached the court soon afterwards. Archer Hou Yi shot down nine suns, leaving one to warm the world.

Emperor Yao was an Emperor devoted to his citizens. He attended ceaselessly to the people's needs and stood by them in their suffering. He lived in a grass hut held together by craggy timber felled from the foot of a mountain. His diet consisted of broth of wild herbs and brown rice. His clothing was made of kudzu hemp. In cold weather he wore a deerskin cape. His dishes were made of earthen clay.

None of this bothered Emperor Yao, since he was constantly only thinking of the people's well-being. His philosophy: "If there is but a single man who goes hungry, it is I who am responsible." Even when someone committed a crime, the emperor blamed his own rule for not being able to prevent the act.

In governance, he had the aid of virtuous ministers such as Qi, who was in charge of war; Lord Millet, the minister of agriculture and ancestor of the Zhou Dynasty (1046–256 BC); and Shun, who had administration powers over education and would become the next emperor. Because Yao's reign was one of virtue and wisdom, the people were able to endure and overcome disasters such as the Great Flood.

The heavens blessed Yao with approval during his reign. Phoenixes, the noblest of birds, perched in the emperor's courtyard. Weeds transformed into cereals, fit for humans to eat.

It is said that Emperor Yao invented the game of Weiqi, also known by its Japanese name of Go. This game has few rules but contains a nearly infinite number of possible scenarios. It has only recently been mastered by artificial intelligence.

Yao created Go hoping to improve the character of his son Dan Zhu, who he believed did not have the morality needed to take on the responsibilities of emperor. Unfortunately, Dan Zhu was arrogant, hot-headed, and unwilling to elevate his characters. Emperor Yao had no choice but to pass on the throne to his minister of education, the wise and honorable Shun.

3
Emperor Shun
Filial and humane

This is the story of Yu Chonghua, a pottery worker who eventually ascended to the imperial throne as the legendary Emperor Shun.

Shun had a terrible childhood. His mother died when he was at a tender age, and his father remarried. The new mother denied Shun any love or kindness and treated him horribly. She had a boy of her own, Xiang, a spoiled child who hated Shun just as much as his mother did.

When Shun was 10 years old, a religious master saw promise in the boy and wanted to teach him to read and write. But Shun's evil stepmother refused, and Shun spent his days working in the fields instead.

However, Shun was unlike other people. He did not bear a grudge against his wicked stepmother or show her disrespect. Instead, he did his best to make his parents' lives better. Heavens were touched by the filial piety* of Shun. An elephant and birds were sent to help him plough and weed the fields respectively.

Shun worked as a potter when he grew up. His great virtues earned him great reputation, so much so that he was recommended to Emperor Yao, who was looking for someone to succeed him. This was during a time when the title of emperor was not hereditary.

Emperor Yao was impressed by Shun after meeting him. He decided to put Shun to the test. He married his two daughters E Huang and Nü Ying to Shun and had his nine sons spend

time with Shun to learn more about this virtuous man. Despite being in Emperor Yao's good books, Shun continued to serve his duties to his stepmother and stepbrother.

However, the stepmother and stepbrother were consumed by jealousy when they saw Shun return home with two elegant princesses as his wives. They conspired against him. Knowing that Shun was an honorable man, they claimed they needed his help before trying to take his life. But Shun's loyal wives protected him with magical powers.

Emperor Yao favored Shun and observed him for 20 years before making him the new emperor. The emperor picked a blessed day to hold his abdication ceremony. He prayed to the heavens for divine approval together with Shun as a gesture that Shun was meant to become the next emperor of China.

They made sacrifices to the gods and sank a piece of fine jade into a river. As soon as this happened, colorful lights beamed from the water, and clouds gathered in the sky. A dragon and a giant tortoise appeared, carrying the heavenly scriptures known as the "River Chart" and the "Inscription of Luo."

Having witnessed these miracles, the emperor abdicated the throne, and Shun was made the new emperor.

Shun treated his people with unconditional compassion and patience, just as he treated his family. He abolished torture and decapitation, and did his best to teach his people about kindness and morality.

* *Filial piety: The concept that people must be good and respectful to their parents and superiors.*

4
Yu the Great
Controls the Flood

Chinese legends say that during the reign of Emperor Yao, much of the world was submerged by a Great Flood. As the flood began, the emperor searched for people to build walls and dams.

Xi Wang Mu, the Lady Queen Mother, informed the emperor that the Flood was ordered by heaven as a punishment for humanity, but the gods had sent a savior: Yu the Great. A title like "the Great" is unusual for a Chinese ruler. But history has made an exception for Yu, who tamed the mighty waters.

It is said that Yu was descended from the Yellow Emperor. His father was Gun (pronounced "gwuhn"), a skilled craftsman. But even his abilities were not good enough to stop the flood, so he took the risk to steal the xi rang, a magical expanding soil, from the gods.

The theft was discovered by the Emperor of Heaven. Enraged, the Emperor of Heaven punished the insolent mortal Gun by sending even stronger torrents. All of Gun's work was destroyed, and he was sentenced to death for stealing from the heavens.

The God of Fire came after him, and Gun died in battle. Emperor Yao had to find someone else to control the waters. He chose Gun's son, the man we now call Yu the Great.

Learning from the mistakes of his father Gun, Yu and his followers worked with the water, instead of against it, so that it would be redirected eastward in an orderly manner. The

ancient records tell of how Yu and his men split open entire mountains to channel the floodwaters back to the ocean.

Yu had two wives, Nü Jiao and Nü You, but he rarely had any time for them. Even when his son was born, Nü Jiao had to bring her child to a boulder hanging over Yu's travel route. Holding the baby, she gazed for a long time as her husband disappeared into the distance.

One story tells how Yu the Great invented chopsticks. One

time, the leader was stuck on an island with some of his men, and became extremely hungry. They found some meat, set up a campfire and prepared their meal, but Yu could hardly wait. Picking up two long sticks, he picked up the meat from the blazing flames. After devouring his meal, he went back to work.

Yu had divine powers, which he sometimes used to work miracles. At the strategic pass of Huanyuan, Yu and his workers ran into some unusually tough stone. Yu the Great grabbed an axe and a drum, and bellowed a command to his men:

"While I am working on this mountain, no one shall disturb me until you hear the sound of the drum."

"Highness, your wives have arrived," an officer replied.

"Wait for me here, I shall come after finishing everything," Yu said. Then he went into the cave and began his task.

When the drum sounded, Nü Jiao and Nü You went up to see their husband. But instead of a man, there in the cave was a huge yellow dragon, slashing away with ease at the solid mountain rock. Yu had taken the form of this majestic beast and his tail hit the drum by accident.

Impressed but terrified, Yu's wives ran out of the cave and back down the mountain.

Yu the Great took over ten years to bring an end to the Great Flood. After this, the reigning Emperor Shun passed on the throne to him.

Before becoming emperor, Yu the Great first offered sacrificial rites to heaven, earth, and the gods. He then prayed to heaven to be granted the wisdom to rule the country.

Emperor Yu founded China's first dynasty, the Xia, and

established the rules of early Chinese government. Instead of ruling the entire country, he gave power to families of nobles who each had their own land. After Yu, Chinese leaders were called kings. China would not have another emperor until Qin Shi Huang.

5
King Wen of Zhou
The Mandate of Heaven

In early Chinese religion, the highest god was Shang Di, Lord of Heaven. Like the Greek god Zeus, he had the power to command lightening. Only royalty had the honor of offering sacrifice and prayer to him on behalf of their people.

Around 3,000 years ago, a Chinese prince was thinking about marriage. There was a woman he loved, but that was not enough. The prince, called Ji Chang, had to be sure that this woman was fit to be queen. Finally, after many rituals and ceremonies, Ji Chang got his answer. His wedding procession crossed a river on a bridge made of boats, and he married the woman he loved, a princess from another kingdom.

Ji Chang became king of Zhou, which was one state in the great feudal realm of the Shang Dynasty. Historians call him King Wen or Wen Wang, which means "king of culture." He ruled responsibly, earning him love and respect. His queen, Tai Si, gave birth to ten sons.

The Shang Dynasty, the second dynasty in Chinese history, had ruled China's states for hundreds of years. Before that had come the Xia, founded by Yu the Great after he stopped the floods.

The king at the time, Di Xin, was a skilled ruler who could hunt wild beasts with his bare hands and win arguments against even the wisest of his ministers. But as Di Xin grew

older, he became a
wasteful tyrant, enjoying fine
food, entertainment, and women inside a grand
palace. He punished those who dared speak out against him,

and raised taxes to support his lifestyle.

Meanwhile, King Wen became more well-known. Nobles and commoners alike praised him for his moral virtue and excellent governance.

Di Xin became jealous. One year, he trapped King Wen by summoning him to the capital, and then throwing him in prison. The Shang tyrant had King Wen's firstborn son, Prince Yikao, put to death.

King Wen accepted his imprisonment. While in captivity, he thought of the Eight Trigrams of divination that the god Fu Xi had passed on to humanity. From these he developed the Sixty-Four Hexagrams, which are contained in the famous Book of Changes.

To save their king, the people of Zhou State sent treasure and beautiful women to Di Xin, hoping that he would have mercy.

After seven years, Di Xin finally released King Wen. By this time, much of China believed that the Shang Dynasty no longer possessed the Mandate of Heaven, or the right to rule the country.

Upon his return, King Wen hired the wise Jiang Ziya to be prime minister, and the Zhou State grew stronger. The king formed alliances with other states.

Time passed. In the year 1056 BC, King Wen passed away. His second son Ji Fa became King Wu or Wu Wang, the "king of war."

In the year 1048 BC, King Wu raised armies to attack Di Xin. Over 800 dukes from around the country offered to join him, but he called off the campaign. The timing wasn't right.

Two years later, Di Xin sent 100,000 elite troops to

subjugate barbarian tribes living in the east. Then one day he received bad news. A massive army from Zhou and its allies was approaching the capital from the west.

The Shang army was large, but its best soldiers were too far away to protect the capital and Di Xin. The frightened king called every able-bodied man to war. Even slaves and criminals were given weapons and sent to fight. The Battle of Muye had begun.

Di Xin's new recruits had no training. They marched into battle, only to flee or surrender. Seeing that all was lost, Di Xin donned a suit of jade armor and retreated to his favorite pavilion. He set fire to his palace and burned himself to death.

In 1046 BC, King Wu united China under the Zhou Dynasty, third in Chinese history. Like the Shang Dynasty, it was a feudal empire composed of many independent states with their own leaders and armies. Most of the new rulers were from the Zhou kingdom or its allies, but some were from the old Shang regime.

King Wu treated the defeated Shang nobles with respect. Some of them did not submit to Zhou's rule and escaped northeast. Led by Ji Zi, they settled in Korea and helped build the Korean nation.

The Zhou Dynasty faced an uncertain future. King Wu died just two years after his victory. His son, King Cheng, was too young to assume leadership over the new empire.

King Wu's younger brother, the Duke of Zhou, decided to run the government in King Cheng's place. Other nobles suspected that he was trying to take power for himself and betray the king, but he withstood the criticism. When King Cheng came of age, the Duke of Zhou kept his promise and gave up control of the empire.

The Zhou Dynasty was the longest dynasty in Chinese history, lasting around 800 years.

The Zhou Dynasty began about 3,000 years ago and lasted almost 800 years until 250 BC It covered the northern and central parts of China's modern territory.

6
Jiang Ziya
Fishing for a king

Like the Trojan War of the ancient Greek world, our memory of early Chinese history is mixed with epic legends. The most well-known stories of how the kingdom of Zhou overthrew the Shang Dynasty come from an epic folk novel Fengshen Yanyi, the Investiture of the Gods.

In the beginning of the novel, Shang King Di Xin, goes to worship the goddess of creation, Nü Wa. Instead of offering his pious respects, Di Xin had lustful thoughts upon seeing Nü Wa's beauty and scribbled an indecent poem on the walls of her temple.

To punish Di Xin, Nü Wa summoned three evil spirits to lead him astray and bring an end to the Shang Dynasty. Meanwhile, other gods began to act. They arranged for kings,

generals, and ministers to play different roles in the unfolding battle between the Shang Dynasty and the kingdom of Zhou.

On Mount Kunlun, in the land of the immortals, there was an aging religious cultivator called Jiang Ziya. His master was a powerful god, Yuanshi Tianzun, or the Respected Primeval Heavenly Elder. He gave Jiang Ziya two tasks. The first was to return to the mortal realm and find a man of righteous character who could help him overthrow Di Xin.

The second duty Jiang had was to invest the gods with titles and ranks according to their conduct in the coming war.

Jiang Ziya went to Zhaoge, capital of the Shang. Two years of searching ended in vain; there was simply no one worthy enough to be endowed with the task of ruling the land. Jiang Ziya decided his task was hopeless and retreated into the wilderness.

One of the spirits Nü Wa sent to entice Di Xin was a fox demon. She possessed the body of a beautiful princess and became the bewitching Da Ji. Once she was in the royal court, she quickly became Di Xin's main consort. The king became even more wasteful and indecent. Many of his ministers and subordinates tried to warn him of the possible dire consequences of his behavior, but he cared about nothing apart from how to satisfy Da Ji.

Da Ji was a perverse character who had an obsession for torturing other people. Under her influence, Di Xin invented cruel methods to torture those against him to death. He killed his queen and replaced her with Da Ji. He had his uncle, the loyal minister Bi Gan, put to death by having his heart cut out.

Many of the princes and kings who served the Shang Dynasty worried about the future. Many of them looked to

King Wen, the leader of the Zhou State. Then Di Xin had King Wen imprisoned for seven years, and his eldest son Yikao was killed.

When King Wen was finally released, he prepared to overthrow the Shang Dynasty. Once, he travelled out into the wild. Someone told him that he would find an ally there.

But instead, he ran into a strange old man muttering to himself while fishing by a river.

Moving closer, King Wen saw that instead of a hook, the old man had a straight nail on the end of his fishing line and was holding it a few feet above the water.

"How can you expect to catch anything?" the surprised king asked.

"Not a problem. The ones who are willing to be hooked will come," the old man said to himself.

King Wen thought the old man must be crazy, but he decided to keep talking to him. It was Jiang Ziya. As their conversation continued, King Wen discovered that Jiang Ziya was no madman, but the person who could help his country to defeat Di Xin and restore order to China.

As for Jiang Ziya, he had finally found the king he was waiting for—not by scouring the land, but by staying put and waiting for him to come.

Jiang Ziya was knowledgeable in military and political affairs, but he also learned formidable supernatural arts that he used to vanquish the gods and demons that went against the will of heaven and continued to assist the Shang Dynasty. One of his great enemies was Shen Gongbao, who was also a student of the Yuanshi Tianzun.

Shen Gongbao was very capable and proud of his ability. He was virtually invincible in combat since he could restore his head even if it was cut off. But when he saw that his master sent Jiang Ziya and not him to fulfill the duty of investing the gods, he was filled with jealousy and acted against Jiang.

The gods defending the Shang Dynasty were eventually defeated. When the evil fox spirit Da Ji was captured, no mortal man ordered to execute her could overcome her seductive magic, until Jiang Ziya himself revealed her true form and beheaded her.

As ordained, Jiang Ziya invested each of the gods who

participated in the heavenly battles with ranks and titles, no matter which side they had fought for. What mattered was their individual courage and virtue.

In history, Jiang Ziya was a real person who served as the prime minister for kings Wen and Wu. His family was given rule over the eastern state of Qi, and it became an important nation during the Spring and Autumn and Warring States periods.

NOTE:

In traditional Chinese folklore, Di Xin, the last king of the Shang Dynasty, is remembered as a wicked and greedy tyrant. Most of the time he is called Zhou Wang, "king of brutality." The Chinese character zhou (紂) used for his name is different from the one used for the kingdom of Zhou (周)

7
King You of Zhou
The laughter of a beauty brings a kingdom to ruin

The Chinese have a saying: a beautiful woman can bring about the downfall of a city or even a nation.

In 780 BC, the capital of the Zhou kingdom was Haojing, a city near present day Xi'an. One summer day, the beacon towers surrounding the capital were set ablaze, signalling that invaders were on the way. Black smoke spewed into the sky.

Rulers of vassal states from all over the kingdom saw the smoke and thought there was an emergency. They got into their armour and marched their men to the royal capital to defend it. But when they arrived at the capital, they saw no enemies, only the king singing and dancing with a gorgeous beauty at his side.

Seeing the soldiers and their generals panting and sweating, expecting a war when there was none, the beauty laughed and gave a bewitching smile.

"Nothing happened, you can go back," the king said.

This was King You of the Zhou, China's third dynasty. He was born in the 750s or 740s BC and made king when he was 13. He was the last king of what historians call the Western Zhou.

The beautiful woman was Bao Si, a stunning but strange woman. King You had a wife, Queen Shen, but he was infatuated with Bao Si's smiles, which were beautiful beyond compare.

But Bao Si had a problem. She would not smile except in the most extraordinary circumstances. King You found it extremely annoying and tried ways and means to make her beam. He demoted Queen Shen and declared that Bao Si's son would inherit the throne. But even that failed to make the lovely woman smile.

King You offered a thousand ounces of gold to anyone who could get Bao Si to laugh. Many came to the king, offering all kinds of strange ideas in hopes of striking it rich. None of the ideas worked.

Other than the vassal states, many tribes in the remote regions did not obey the royal court in Haojing. They did not know about agriculture and lived by hunting or raiding the riches of civilized folk. The vassal rulers of the Zhou Dynasty looked down on them and called them the Di and Rong barbarians.

The beacon towers that surrounded Haojing served as a giant fence around the capital city. When the Di and Rong tribes launched an attack, beacons would be lit to send out smoke signals. Vassal rulers from near and far would see the smoke and come to the rescue of the capital and crush the invaders.

This was all well and good until someone suggested charming the lady with the flames and splendour. So King You took Bao Si to the summit of Mount Li to enjoy the spectacle.

Sure enough, the scene of the beacon towers all ablaze was an impressive sight to behold, and Bao Si, who was usually bored, was amused and delighted. King You was satisfied and felt a sense of accomplishment.

When the rulers of the vassal states arrived to see not the

enemy but King You drinking and making merry with Bao Si, no one dared voice their exasperation. They just returned home quietly.

As King You repeated the antic again and again, the rulers grew tired of the trick.

Finally, the barbarian hordes did arrive to attack Haojing and loot its riches. But this time, the flare of the beacon roused no reaction from the rulers of the vassal states. King

You was killed together with his guards, the royal capital was seized, and Bao Si was taken away by the invaders.

The Zhou Dynasty did not end with the death of King You. Ping, the son of Queen Shen, escaped east along the Yellow River to Luoyang, where the new capital was established. Since it was located east of Haojing, the new dynasty was called the Eastern Zhou.

Things were no longer the same. The vassal leaders still respected King Ping as their lord, but the dynasty lost the authority it had in King You's day. The vassals acted more like independent states, and even began to fight wars with one another instead of going to the king to settle their disputes. This was the start of China's Spring and Autumn and Warring States eras, lasting over 500 years between 789 and 221 BC.

When the Western Zhou Dynasty fell, a secretary in the state of Lu wrote down the events as they happened at the time. This marked the beginning of the valuable Chinese tradition of putting down history in official documents.

Since about 2,800 years ago, historians have been documenting all major events in Chinese history, making China the civilization with the longest continuously recorded history.

8
Lao Zi
The Old Master of Taoism

*I*t was the 6th century BC Officer Yin Xi stood guard with his men at the Gate of Hangu, the western border of ancient China. Looking east, he noticed a mystical violet aura approaching. It was a good omen. A great sage was near.

Sure enough, an old man riding a water buffalo soon arrived. He was none other than Lao Zi—the Old Master. He was about to leave China after years of teaching.

Yin Xi begged Lao Zi to leave behind some of his wisdom, and the sage eventually agreed. He stayed at the gatehouse and began writing.

Lao Zi was a librarian of the royal library of the Zhou Dynasty. According to legend, he achieved immortality through self-cultivation, and he had many followers who called him "Old Master" because of his very advanced age.

Lao Zi's book, the *"Tao Te Ching"*, became the central text of Taoism, the Chinese philosophy of the Tao or Way. Practitioners of Taoism believe in living simple lives and following the natural order, instead of specific rules. Lao Zi wrote, "There is one thing that exists even before the universe, revolving without end or exhaustion. I do not know its name, so I call it the 'Tao.'"

The first line of the *"Tao Te Ching"* says, "The Tao that can be explained is not the permanent Tao."

There are many stories that characterize Lao Zi and his teachings.

One day, Lao Zi came to the city of Kaifeng. When he dismounted from his black water buffalo, he came across his student Yang Ziju, whose house was nearby.

"I have purchased land in this area where my ancestors lived," said Yang. "I've started construction on my new residence, and I direct my servants to do their chores about the house. I have also established various rules to put the whole family in order."

The Old Master asked, "Don't you already have a place to live? Why are you going to all this trouble?"

Yang replied, "We religious cultivators need a quiet environment to sit in meditation. We need to be relaxed when walking, we need clean and refreshing tea and food and we don't want to be bothered by noises when sleeping. How can we meet these demands without a large house and many servants?"

Lao Zi laughed and said: "There is no need for a great mansion with a large band of servants. Just eat when you are hungry, rest when you are tired, rise when the sun rises and sleep when it sets."

"Great wisdom is natural," Lao Zi said. "You don't need to create calmness by forcing the world to be calm. Without any particular desire in mind, we can still be calm even as we walk. Without particular care in regard to what we eat, our food will be clean and healthy naturally. Getting rid of unnecessary desires means we can sleep in peace no matter where we are."

As they crossed a river, Lao Zi told Yang Ziju, "You hold your head high and stick your chest out, giving others a proud and self-absorbed look. When a gentleman is with commoners, he should fit in naturally like a block of ice melting into water. When working with others, you should be modest like a servant."

Upon hearing that, Yang Ziju corrected his arrogant manner. He strived to be modest and respectful and stopped discriminating against people in terms of wealth and background.

Gengsang Chu was another follower of Lao Zi's. He was conscious of his behavior and way of living and brought great benefits to his village, where he had been living for three years.

The men ploughed the fields and there was always enough for the people to eat. The women wove and there was always enough clothing to be worn. Everyone put in his or her best efforts and got along in peace. The people were so happy that they wanted to make Gengsang Chu their lord.

To everyone's surprise, Gengsang did not like the idea at all. In fact he became so upset that he almost wanted to leave.

He explained, "Nature shows us that the bird never rejects the high sky, the beast does not abandon its woodland habitat, and the fish does not escape its watery depths. That is their way of life."

"It is the same for people. For those of us who practise cultivation, we are like everyone else. We do not fear that we are poor or that our station is too low. Please do not ask me to be your lord."

The *"Tao Te Ching"* has only five thousand words, but its wisdom has guided people across Asia for generations. Taoism has coexisted with other Chinese beliefs and religions for thousands of years.

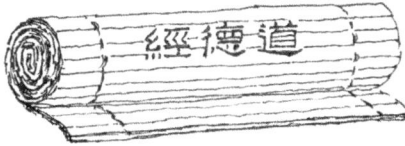

Confucius, known as the greatest teacher in all of Chinese history, tried to improve the world by conducting lessons on ancient customs. However, he gained much deeper wisdom through his conversations with Lao Zi.

"To rule this world, you must study the spirit of water," Lao Zi told him. "It benefits everything, but it is soft. It stays in the lowest position and does not compete with other things. There is no need to spend every day debating moral theories. If you are like water, people may learn the principles of nature from you."

Confucius travelled back to his homeland, the state of Lu. His disciples were eager to find out what he had learned.

"I can see the birds flying and the fish swimming," Confucius said. "Beasts walk and they can be caught in nets. Fish can be angled for on hooks and birds in flight can be shot down. But the dragon! It rides the winds and clouds to the highest point of heaven. It is impossible to catch it. That is Lao Zi!"

9

Confucius
China's greatest teacher

"A righteous person can guard his morality and virtue even in times of hardship, but a wicked person will commit evil once he suffers misfortune."

Perhaps no one has influenced Asian culture so much as Kong Qiu, better known as Master Kong or by the name given to him by Europeans—Confucius.

Confucius was born in 551 BC at the end of the Spring and Autumn Period during the Eastern Zhou Dynasty. Sometimes he worked as an official, but his main talent was teaching. He had a total of 3,000 students, of whom 72 became outstanding sages. Many of Confucius' lessons came from conversations he had with his disciples as they travelled across different parts of China.

Confucius was on the way to the state of Qi with his loyal disciple Zilu. One day, they passed by Mount Tai and saw a woman weeping by a gravestone. Confucius sent Zilu to find out what had happened. The woman told Zilu: "There is a tiger on this mountain. First, it ate my father. Not long ago, it devoured my husband. Now it has killed my son!"

"Why don't you move to a different place?" Confucius asked with concern.

The woman replied, "There may be tigers here, but there are no oppressive officials."

Confucius sighed deeply and said to Zilu: "Remember this!

Tyranny is fiercer than a tiger."

During the Eastern Zhou Dynasty (770–221 BC), China still had a king, but the real power was split among many different states that fought with each other for dominance.

Confucius believed that society was in chaos because people no longer followed traditional customs. He explained that different people—such as rulers and subjects, parents and children, or husbands and wives—could only respect and cooperate with each other if they followed the a set of rules and values known as *li*, a word that means etiquette or ritual.

Besides the emphasis on ritual, Confucius also gave special importance to the supreme virtue, *xiao*, translated as filial piety or respect for elders. Confucius believed that filial piety was the basis of all proper human action, including kindness, justice, and loyalty.

Many of Confucius' teachings and sayings are similar to those found in Western religions and philosophy. Jesus taught the Christians to do unto others what they would want done to themselves, and Confucius said: "What you do not want done to yourself, do not do to others."

Confucius lived and taught around the same time as the great philosophers of ancient Greece. Plato said that ideals are invisible but do not change, whereas material reality is visible but not permanent. If Plato and Confucius had met, they would probably have agreed with each other.

Confucius was on a trip with his students one day when one of them became ill. His disciple Zilu was shocked at the fact that even someone who followed righteousness could get sick. But to Confucius, suffering was an important test of true character.

"A righteous person would uphold his principles even in times of hardship," he told Zilu. "But a wicked person would commit evil when he suffers misfortune."

Confucius taught people that they should act responsibly and not just to satisfy their emotions.

One of his disciples was Zigong, a man of great wealth. On his way to accept a government position in the state of Lu, Zigong came across a few slaves from Lu. He used some of his money to pay for their freedom and helped them return home.

In order to increase its population, the government of Lu was offering rewards to those who freed Lu slaves living in other states. To further demonstrate his virtue, Zigong refused to accept the money, saying he did not need it.

When Confucius heard about this, he criticized Zigong for setting an impossible example for the commoners: "Most of the people in Lu State are poor. If all of them consider it improper to accept a reward for buying the freedom of a slave, nobody can afford to do that."

Over the centuries, the teachings of Confucius became more popular and were supported by Chinese rulers. Confucianism is known as *Rujiao* in Chinese, a word that actually means "the religion of rituals."

Confucius collected writings from around the country and edited them into classics that represented his beliefs. There were six books in total, but one, the "Classic of Music", was lost in later generations. Today they are known as the Five Classics of Confucianism, namely the "Classic of Poetry", the "Book of Documents", the "Book of Rites", the "Classic of Change", and the "Spring and Autumn Annals".

Unlike most faiths, Confucius focused on secular morality, not gods and the supernatural. But he believed that part of living a proper life was to worship the spirits of one's ancestors.

Confucius gained much of his wisdom from Lao Zi, the great master of the Taoist religion.

"I'm an ungifted student," Confucius said upon meeting the Old Master." Though my mind is clear and I have studied diligently, I have made many pointless travels, and I still haven't found the key to great wisdom like yours. Please show me the way to enlightenment!"

Lao Zi said: "To learn the fundamentals of the Great Tao, you must learn to see the common roots that exist in all things. At the formation of the universe, everything was the same to begin with, and all distinctions were created only afterwards. Only by seeing how they are alike will you understand the Tao."

At first glance, Taoism is the opposite of Confucianism. Its cultivators follow the natural way and practice non-intention, while Confucius taught his disciples to establish rules to protect morality.

However, when he met with Lao Zi, Confucius discovered that his teachings were actually encompassed within the formless principles of Taoism. The rituals and filial piety of Confucianism were just tools for common people living in everyday society. The world was always changing, and the rules of society could not stay the same forever. Through cultivation, a Taoist practitioner could achieve a high spiritual level and exist in harmony with heaven, earth, and man.

Suddenly Confucius was inspired. He said: "At age 30, I established myself. At age 40, I became clear about my place in the world; but only now, at the age of 50, am I aware of the natural law!"

10
Guan Zhong and Duke Huan
Honor the king, expel the barbarians

It happened in 685 BC. An assassin lay in wait as a procession of horses and carriages of the state of Qi hurried along the Yellow River. When the horses approached, he stepped out of a grove, drew an arrow, and shot it right at his enemy, a young aristocrat. The arrow hit the young man in the chest, and he crumpled in his carriage.

The assassin was Guan Zhong. He fled quickly, but we will be seeing more of him.

The young nobleman with an arrow in his chest was Jiang Xiaobai, and he was in a life-or-death race against his brother Jiang Jiu to get back to the Qi capital, where the throne stood empty. Their father, the Duke of Qi, had been murdered a year before and replaced by a fake duke, forcing the brothers to go into hiding.

Now the fake duke had passed away as well, and the first of the real duke's sons to return to Qi would mount the throne. Xiaobai had gotten a head start, and Jiu had to act fast. Guan Zhong, one of his servants, volunteered himself for the mission to kill Xiaobai.

Guan Zhong was a skilled archer, and he made certain he hit his target. He thought that he had shot Xiaobai in the heart when he saw the latter spit out blood.

Jiu breathed a sigh of relief upon hearing the news. The demise of his brother meant the throne was in the bag.

It took just a split second for Xiaobai to realize that someone had tried to assassinate him. He bit his tongue, spat out blood and crumpled into a heap in order to deceive the assassin that he was killed. His men continued on their way to the state of Qi with his "body" in tow.

Xiaobai reached Qi ahead of Jiu and ascended the throne as Duke Huan of Qi. The first thing he did was announce plans to invade the neighboring state of Lu, where Jiu and Guan Zhong were hiding. The officials of Lu were terrified and immediately had Jiu put to death. Guan Zhong, the assassin was extradited back to Qi so the duke could personally administer punishment. War was averted.

As Guan Zhong returned to Qi in shackles, he wondered how much longer he would live. But to his surprise, as soon as he crossed the border, the soldiers removed his shackles and helped him into a beautiful carriage fit for a king.

Why did Duke Huan forgive him? Guan Zhong could have been beheaded, but his friend Bao Shuya, a trusted advisor to Duke Huan, admonished the latter to keep Guan Zhong alive.

Bao Shuya saw that Guan Zhong had great abilities and potential. "If you want to rule one state, I will suffice. But if you wish to govern the world, use Guan Zhong."

Duke Huan received Guan Zhong at his palace. The punishment he "personally administered" was to offer Guan Zhong the position of chief minister.

In a famous conversation, Duke Huan asked Guan Zhong, "If I want a prosperous nation and stable society, how should I go about it?"

"The first thing is to gain the people's support," Guan Zhong replied.

"How do we make the people support us?" the duke asked.

Guan Zhong said, "To gain the support of the people, we should take care of them. If the duke is able to care for his subjects, they will be willing to contribute to the country without you ordering them to. When the people are rich, they will be easy to govern. It is often the case that a peaceful country is wealthy while a chaotic country is impoverished. This is a self-evident truth."

"But with the people well-fed and well-clothed, how will we

recruit soldiers for our armies?" the duke asked.

"We should value our troops' quality over their numbers," Guan Zhong said. "With high morale and good training, we need not worry about their fighting ability."

"What happens when our people are rich and our armies well-trained, but the government has no money?"

"Develop forestry, develop salt mines. Build foundries and fisheries. The whole country's income will increase. Help business grow, and you will get the wealth of the world by trading. The taxes from all this will certainly be enough to maintain our armies."

This talk interested Duke Huan. "A rich nation means a powerful army. Doesn't this mean we can achieve world domination?"

"Do not get too excited just yet, milord," Guan Zhong cautioned. "Mastery of the earth is a great undertaking. We cannot act rashly. Our biggest priority now is to improve the lives of our people and enrich the nation. If we cannot even do that, it is useless to think about dominion over anything."

Guan Zhong overhauled the management of Qi. The moral code he invented for the whole country was called *"li yi lian chi"* (禮義廉恥), which historians often translate as "propriety, justice, integrity, and honor."

"Propriety" meant that people had to treat others politely and follow national customs. "Justice" meant that they had to treat each other fairly. "Integrity" meant they had to think for the good of all instead of wallowing in their own greed. Finally, "honor" meant that the people had to know good from evil and feel shame when they did something wrong.

These were not just nice-sounding words. Guan Zhong

needed everyone to be on the same page if he was going to make Duke Huan run China. Propriety, justice, integrity, and honor, he said, were the four pillars of the state. Losing even one could bring the state of Qi to its knees.

Propriety, justice, integrity, and honor helped Guan Zhong reform agriculture, artisanship, trade, military training and recruitment, and community management.

Qi was one of the first states in China to keep track of its people and organize them for work, military service, and taxes. Five families formed one *gui*, which literally means "track." Ten tracks were called a *li*, which is also a Chinese word for "mile." Four *li* (200 families) were a *lian*, which is similar to a company in the military. The biggest was a *xiang*, which simply means "town." It included ten companies for a total of 2,000 families.

In wartime, each household was responsible for producing one man for the army. Five towns, with 10,000 men called up for service, made an army under the command of a marshal.

In peacetime, military training was held every spring and autumn. Men from the same tracks, miles, companies, and towns trained together. Not only did this save time, it also filled them with brotherly spirit and pumped up their morale during real combat.

Guan Zhong ran the state of Qi like a business. He lowered taxes and tied them with the fertility of the land, so that farmers with bad land or a poor harvest would not be burdened too much. At the same time, it was strictly forbidden for rich people or government officials to take a farmer's land without permission.

In those days, most people were farmers. The agricultural policy was especially important. Guan Zhong understood economics and set up a national food bank. If there was a bumper harvest, the government would buy up excess grain for storage to increase its price and encourage farmers to keep working hard. When the harvest was poor, the government would sell the grain it stored to keep prices lower and prevent the poor from starvation.

Merchant business and special industries like salt mining or ironworks were taxed more to make up for the lower land taxes.

Qi was soon the richest state in China. The humane government policies attracted immigrants from many foreign kingdoms, boosting Qi's population greatly.

Guan Zhong knew that the King of the Zhou Dynasty was weak and needed support, so he advised Duke Huan to pay the king the greatest respect and honor him by following the ancient rituals.

Because of Qi's power, historians consider it the first hegemonic state of the Spring and Autumn Era. It was Duke Huan's responsibility to make sure the other states obeyed and consulted the king. Every so often, a summit of all major leaders was held to review the laws among the states and make sure that they were being followed. States that violated the laws were invaded and punished by the Qi army.

Barbarians from outside China were becoming a threat at this time. Rulers of other states relied on Duke Huan's strength to keep wild tribes from attacking their towns and villages, although some of them were jealous of his power.

Honoring the king and expelling the barbarians, known in Chinese as "zun wang rang yi" (尊王攘夷), was one of Guan Zhong's biggest accomplishments. Hundreds of years later, Confucius said, "If it were not for Guan Zhong, today we would be wearing our hair and clothes in wild tribal fashion."

Guan Zhong was a businessman by training and knew how to use the economy to bring down other states. Between the states of Qi and Lu was a minor kingdom called Hengshan. It was home to skilled craftsmen who made all kinds of weapons and military equipment. Guan Zhong used Qi's massive cash reserves to buy up whatever Hengshan could produce at the highest prices possible.

When other states saw what was happening, they assumed that the state of Qi was preparing for a war and also bought arms from Hengshan. For a while, Hengshan enjoyed massive profits because of the increased price of weaponry. The state ordered its people to cut down large numbers of trees for timber to keep up weapon production.

A year later, Qi began buying food from all around China, paying double the normal price.

Seventeen months into the plan, Qi suddenly stopped buying military equipment from Hengshan. Profits from the war industry fell instantly, and the people of Hengshan who had stopped growing enough food to feed themselves were now in danger of starvation. In less than a year, the entire country begged to become a part of Qi State.

Guan Zhong used a similar plan to deal with the state of Lu. This time, he advised Duke Huan to buy up all the popular royal clothing that was being produced in Lu. This led the people of Lu to stop planting grain and replace their crops with mulberry, hemp, and cotton—the plants needed for textile manufacturing. After raising the price of luxury clothing, the state of Qi suddenly banned its people from wearing these clothes and forbade the sale of food to the state of Lu.

There was an immediate hike in the price of food in Lu, over 10 times its price in Qi. Even if all the farmers in Lu replanted grain, it would still be five months before they could collect a new harvest. On the brink of starvation, Lu had no choice but to surrender to Qi.

At a time when the Zhou Dynasty king was too weak to govern the land, Qi safeguarded Chinese civilization from destruction. Using both military force and economic methods, Duke Huan and Guan Zhong maintained a stable "international order" for around 30 years.

In 645 BC, Guan Zhong fell ill. Knowing that his days were numbered, he advised Duke Huan on how to keep winning in war and trade.

Duke Huan wanted to replace his dying minister with Bao Shuya, the man who had grown up with Guan Zhong and saved his life years before. But Guan Zhong knew he was not right for the job.

"Bao Shuya is quite the gentleman," Guan Zhong said, "but his ideas about right and wrong are too strict. If he sees someone committing a wrong deed, he will not be able to work with him. It's impossible to do politics this way."

Duke Huan then named three candidates, who he thought were his loyal subjects. But there was a problem. These men were a bit too loyal, even to the extent of neglecting their parents and killing their children just to please the duke. Guan Zhong warned that they had poor moral character and were best kept away from power.

Duke Huan seemed to agree, but he did not take Guan Zhong's words to heart. A few years after Guan Zhong died, all three of the men he had warned against were promoted to high offices.

One day, they led a group of nobles to overthrow Duke Huan. The traitors built an impenetrable brick wall around the palace and trapped the duke inside. Surrounded by the clamor of the richest city in China, the poor duke was starved to death.

Qi remained a powerful state, but it was nothing like its old self under Duke Huan and Guan Zhong. Throughout the Spring and Autumn Period, other states would gain and lose the envied status of hegemon. In the end, they declared themselves independent kingdoms, prepared to fight to the death to unify China under a new dynasty.

As the Zhou kingdom became weaker, Qi State was the first state to become a Hegemon among the Chinese nations.

11
Wu Zixu
Revenge and justice

At the end of the Spring and Autumn Period around 2,500 years ago, the Wu family lived in the state of Chu, serving the royal court.

Wu She, the father of Wu Zixu, was a royal tutor to the crown prince of Chu.

King Ping, the ruler of Chu, arranged for his son to marry a beautiful princess from Qin. But when the lustful king laid eyes on her, he was captivated by her beauty and decided to keep her for himself. A fight in the imperial court broke out, and suddenly the tutor Wu She found himself in prison because of his relationship to the prince.

Wu Zixu and his elder brother Wu Shang knew that they would be the next victims and fled to the countryside. King Ping was apprehensive about that. He came up with a plan to get rid of the Wu family in one go.

He made Wu She write a letter to his sons, begging them to come back and visit him in the capital. His intention was to kill all three of them.

The brothers knew it was a trap. But to disobey their father was a terrible sin, and allowing their family to be wiped out was equally sinful.

Finally, the brothers found a solution—Wu Shang would go back to the capital, even though that would mean he would be killed together with his father. This would be how they could fulfill their duties to their father.

True enough, Wu Shang was put to death with Wu She. As the only survival, Wu Zixu's only purpose in life was to seek justice by eliminating the kingdom of Chu.

He became a marked man. King Ping mobilized his armies and sentries to seal off roads and mountain passes. Soldiers were patrolling the roads and watching the borders. It was impossible for Wu Zixu to escape from the country, let alone return with an army of his own. He would need a lot of skill and luck to cross the border.

Along the way, Wu Zixu ran into an old friend, Officer Shen Baoxu. As Shen prepared to arrest him, Wu begged for mercy and explained why it was his duty to defeat the state of Chu.

"Very well," Shen Baoxu said. "You may leave and complete your quest to conquer Chu."

"But know this: I will revive the kingdom even after its defeat."

Wu Zixu bade farewell to Shen Baoxu and made his escape from Chu. At the mountain pass of Zhaoguan, he panicked, knowing that the guards at the checkpoint would recognize him. For days and nights, he did not know what to do, and his hair turned gray from stress. He became so haggard that he passed through the checkpoint without being caught.

Wu Zixu then crossed the mighty Yangtze River, hiding among the reeds to avoid detection. Finally, he arrived in the eastern state of Wu. He had no money, no friends, just the clothes on his back and his indomitable spirit.

By some stroke of luck, the prince of Wu spotted Wu Zixu during a tour. Surprised by Wu Zixu's noble manner even in utter poverty, the prince invited him to his abode. After a few conversations, the prince found Wu to be an extraordinary person, and recommended him to serve as an advisor to the king.

The prince had his own problems though. He was the rightful heir to the throne, but the usurper King Liao and his sons were in control of the court.

When Wu Zixu saw that the prince was being done an injustice, he quit his new job and went to the countryside to become a farmer. Meanwhile, he waited for the prince to seize the throne that was his birthright.

The prince found two dedicated men who came up with daring plans to kill the king and his son. The assassins accomplished their missions but lost their lives. The prince ascended the throne and became King Helü of Wu.

Wu Zixu was the new king's most trusted advisor. He had such authority and ability that he founded and built the city of Suzhou, located near Shanghai.

Wu Zixu also introduced to Helü a military strategist from the state of Qi, Sun Wu. He was none other than Sun Zi, author of the world-famous Art of War. The knowledge in this book is still used today.

Sun Zi divided the military wisdom he gained over the years into thirteen components, and presented it to King Helü in detail. Helü was impressed and made Sun the commander of his army.

In 506 BC, Wu Zixu got his revenge. Over 60,000 Wu soldiers, under the command of Sun Zi and vice-command of Wu Zixu, marched their way to the state of Chu. The Wu troops were unstoppable. Following five consecutive defeats, the Chu forces lost all will to fight and Wu's soldiers soon conquered the capital.

King Ping of Chu, who killed Wu Zixu's father and brother, was already dead. Wu Zixu dug up his body, whipped it three hundred times, and cut off the head.

King Ping's son, the crown prince, was murdered around the time when Wu Zixu's family was executed. His son was still alive though, so Sun Zi advised King Helü to place him on the Chu throne. This way, the people of Chu would not feel that they had been treated unfairly.

But the king ignored this advice, and foolishly tried to turn the territory of Chu into a part of Wu. The people of Chu were angry, and the other states were aware of it. Shen Baoxu, the friend of Wu Zixu who had let him go many years before, now saw his chance to revive his homeland. He travelled to the state of Qin and knelt before the royal palace for seven days and seven nights.

His devotion and loyalty finally moved the duke of Qin, who sent his best troops to help the Chu nobility mount a counterattack against Wu. After ten months of occupying the Chu capital, the Wu troops eventually retreated. The king of Chu then returned from hiding. With the help of Shen Baoxu, they reconstructed their homeland from ruins.

Wu Zixu continued to serve King Helü as minister of the state of Wu, winning many victories for him and his son, King Fuchai. The state of Wu grew more powerful and dominated many nations to the west and north. But the real danger came from an unsuspected enemy.

12
King Goujian of Yue
The triumph of a defeated kingdom

In the last chapter, we saw how the Wu State conquered the much larger Chu kingdom. Yue was a tribal nation neighboring Wu, and its rulers constantly created disturbance along the border.

In one battle, the Yue troops used a surprise tactic and killed Wu's leader, King Helü.

The new king of Wu State, Fuchai, was intelligent and gifted in music and literature. As his father Helü lay dying from his wounds in battle, Fuchai vowed to avenge him and destroy the state of Yue, for it was their soldiers who had dealt him this mortal blow.

Worried that he might forget the last will of his father, King Fuchai ordered a soldier to stand by his bed and shout to him every morning: "Fuchai, have you forgotten that Yue State slew your father?"

Fuchai waited for his opportunity. In 494 BC, Wu and Yue fought a large battle and Wu won a glorious victory.

Goujian, the king of Yue State, fled to a mountain near Yue's capital with his last men. Cornered by Wu's troops, Goujian pulled up his sword wanting to kill himself, but his guards and two ministers stopped him.

The two ministers were Fan Li and Wen Zhong. They said to Goujian: "It's very easy to die, but to reconstruct a country is incredibly difficult. Do you want to choose the easier road and end as a loser, or do you want to stay strong until you see success?"

In order to preserve Yue's people, land, soldiers, and strength, he signed a humiliating surrender document and agreed to personally become a slave for King Fuchai of Wu.

Meanwhile, the Yue government continued to operate under the two ministers. They bribed government officials in the Wu State with large amounts of money and behaved humbly to please them. They also gathered the most beautiful girls of Yue and sent them to live in King Fuchai's palaces.

The most elegant woman among these beauties was Xi Shi, one of China's Four Great Beauties. She was said to be so dazzling that as she combed her hair along the river, the fish

would sink to the river bottom in shame.

Xi Shi's beauty became Yue State's secret weapon. It was said that the Yue minister Fan Li was Xi Shi's instructor and fell in love with her, but he sacrificed his love to serve his homeland and presented Xi Shi to King Fuchai all the same. Fuchai was instantly bewitched and spent all his time with her.

Meanwhile, King Goujian worked like a dog in the palace of Wu. He did everything possible to serve Fuchai—when Fuchai fell ill, Goujian pretended to be so anxious that he even tasted his master's feces to determine the cause.

Fuchai was moved by Goujian's humble attitude; not to mention, many of the king's ministers had been influenced by the humble Yue servants and their gifts. Over time Fuchai heard lots of praise for Yue and its people.

Three years after Goujian became a slave, Fuchai forgave their past conflicts and set him free.

But Goujian had war on his mind. Returning to his country, the king did not sleep in his palace, but continued his simple servant's lifestyle. His bed was hard and made of straw, and above it he hung the bitter gallbladder of a snake. Every day Goujian woke up and licked it to remind himself of the shame and humiliation of being a slave—and what he was going to do to avenge it.

All this time, King Fuchai assumed that Yue State was a loyal ally, so he focused on attacking and dominating other countries to the north. The easy victories Fuchai gained with the help of the master of war, Sun Zi, made him arrogant and conceited. Not once did he suspect any danger.

The danger didn't escape the eyes of his two loyal advisors. Sun Zi saw that Fuchai did not want to hear his advice, so he retired and left the country. Wu Zixu, however, tried to convince the king to correct his ways.

Instead, Wu Zixu's advice became totally unwelcome. Forgetting how this man had once helped his father, King Helü, come to power in Wu and bring down the mighty Chu State, Fuchai called Wu Zixu an "old devil" and ordered him to commit suicide.

Before Wu Zixu slit his throat, he asked that his eyes be torn out and placed on the southern gate of Wu's capital. He was sure that Fuchai's actions would lead to disaster, and wanted to be able to see the day that the armies of Yue marched triumphantly into Wu.

As a vassal state, Yue offered its best rice to Wu. This was another trick. The rice was intentionally steamed and dried, so when Wu's peasants planted it in their field, nothing would grow. The people of Wu faced starvation.

In 482 BC, Fuchai again went to central China to show off his strength in front of the other feudal leaders. Leaping at the opportunity, Goujian made an unexpected raid on Wu's capital, killing Fuchai's son and royal heir.

As Fuchai marched back, he found himself facing with a formidable and vengeful army. Being no match to Yue, Fuchai bought temporary peace at a hefty price.

A decade later in 473 BC, Goujian returned with even stronger troops, encircling Gusu, the capital of Wu. The siege lasted for three years. Seeing no hope of winning the war, Fuchai asked to surrender, offering to become a servant for Goujian. Goujian was not so forgiving. As the Yue troops broke through the city wall, Fuchai went to the highest mountain, drew a sword, and killed himself.

As he died, Fuchai covered his eyes in shame. He did not

want to face Wu Zixu, whose advice he had ignored, when he traveled into the afterlife.

After conquering Wu, Goujian found Fuchai's sword and wore it personally, naming it the Sword of Goujian.

In 1972, an excavation found the sword in an ancient tomb in Hebei Province. The sword was bending over 30 degrees under collapsed stone, but it miraculously snapped back into its original shape when it was removed from the ruins. The sword, which slept underground for over 2,400 years, was still sharp and untarnished. A test by archaeologists found that it could easily cut through 42 paper sheets with one slice.

After years of war and struggle, Goujian couldn't adjust to peacetime.

During the final battle for Wu's capital, the minister Fan Li, who had always been at Goujian's side, suddenly disappeared. Also missing was the beauty Xi Shi. Soon, Wen Zhong received a letter from Fan Li.

Fan wrote, "King Goujian has a long, skinny face and a nose hooked like an eagle's beak. You can go through adversity and hardship with him, but not prosperity and happiness." Fan Li encouraged Wen Zhong to escape.

Wen Zhong disregarded his friend's warning. During the most difficult times he dedicated his whole heart to help Goujian revive the country. He was a loyal minister and had nothing to fear.

But as Fan Li predicted, trouble soon came. Wen Zhong had come up with seven strategies to undermine and destroy the formidable Wu State, and ended up using five of them. The fact that one person could have such great power both impressed and terrified Goujian. Within three years Goujian decided to get rid of Wen Zhong and forced him to commit suicide.

Meanwhile, Fan Li had escaped north to become a merchant in the state of Qi, where it is said that he had brought Xi Shi and lived in peace with her. He made lots of money, but donated everything he didn't need.

In the following centuries, most of the Yue people mixed with the Chinese from the north, while others continued south and became the Min Yue and Nan Yue. Some believe that Vietnam, which is called Yue Nan in Chinese, was established by their descendants.

13
Mo Zi
Strong defense, universal love

I n the 400s BC, the southern Chinese kingdom of
Chu mobilized its national forces to attack the small
neighboring state of Song. The royal palace guard
informed King Hui of Chu that a man dressed in worn and
shabby clothing, who called himself Mo Di, was standing
outside and demanding an audience with the king.

Mo Di was quite famous and had many dedicated
followers. Many of them were even willing to give their lives
for him. King Hui invited him into the palace.

King Hui addressed Mo Di respectfully. "Sir, why are you
dressed in tattered clothes and shoes that are falling apart?"

"I heard that Your Majesty is preparing troops to invade the
state of Song," said Mo Di. "For the sake of your distinguished
nation, I have spent ten days and ten nights travelling here
from Song and only just arrived. I beg Your Majesty to forgive
my recklessness, but the matter is so urgent that I needed to
meet Your Majesty immediately."

The king knew at once that Mo Di had come from Song to
stop his invasion plans. He replied: "Sir, you need not speak
further. The state of Song has been very disrespectful to me
and to our state, so we must punish them."

Mo Di said: "I am an ordinary man, not a noble. I'm not
familiar with international politics. There are just a few things
I'd like to ask you."

He continued: "Imagine such a person: his house is

splendidly built, and he has great wealth. Not only does he wear fine clothes, but he also gets to eat meat every day. Yet he has the strange desire to steal from his neighbor, a poor man who lives in a small house, dresses in plain clothing, and eats bland food. How would Your Majesty judge such a person?"

King Hui replied that the person Mo Di had just described must be mentally ill.

"The state of Chu is a great power," Mo Di said. "Its territory and population are huge, and it enjoys much wealth as well. The state of Song, on the other hand, is poor and small. To make war on Song just because Chu feels Song is not showing respect is clearly irrational and not worth the cost."

King Hui could not refute Mo Di, but he insisted on declaring war.

Mo Di then warned the king that the Chu army may be large and powerful, but Song's cities were well-defended by tough walls and fortresses. It would be a hard battle if Chu chose to attack.

King Hui argued: "I have the famed engineer Lu Ban on my side. He can build all kinds of equipment needed for breaking fortifications. My army will definitely be victorious."

"I grew up with Lu Ban," Mo Di said. "It's been a long time since I last saw him. If Your Majesty could send for him, we can enact the coming battle. We'll see if his siege engines can defeat the city walls of Song."

The king summoned Lu Ban. The two of them simulated various kinds of battles using miniature figures. Lu Ban represented the attacking Chu army, and Mo Di played the part of the Song defenses. Mo Di won every round.

Lu Ban sighed. "It seems I'm no match for Mo Di, but I

know how Chu can still win."

The king asked him what the method was, but Lu Ban refused to speak further.

Mo Di filled in for him: "I know what the method is: to kill me right now and prevent me from going back to lead Song's defenses. But this will not work either, since my 300 students are already in Song and they have learnt the tactics I've devised. It would still be impossible for Chu to win the war."

King Hui thought for a long time. In the end, he decided that victory was not likely. He cancelled the entire campaign.

At that time, Mo Di was 29 years old. He was renowned throughout China as a scholar and engineer. He is respectfully known as Mo Zi, which means "Master Mo."

Mo Zi was a great philosopher, military expert, and scientist. It is still unknown where he was born. Though he lived well over 2,000 years ago, his ideas about equality, "universal love," and pacifism are similar to

modern ideas about egalitarianism. Mo Zi's idea of universal love meant that in addition to their families, people should love strangers too. He was against violence and warfare unless it was in self-defense.

Mo Zi and his students created the basis for many Chinese weapons. His 100 most famous students were all engineers. They devised various war machines, such as a crossbow car and a revolving arrow gun. Mo Zi even built a flying wooden model of a hawk. He used the mechanical principle of levers to produce the world's first crane. It was capable of lifting stones weighing several hundred kilograms.

Most importantly, however, Mo Zi gathered civil engineers from around the country to form a semi-secret group consisting of several thousand people. They studied not just industrial methods but also martial arts. They helped the leaders of many countries around China construct defenses. They took orders from no government and followed only the philosophical principles that Mo Zi taught.

The group was often banned and forced to operate underground. Mo Zi's original community of engineers and martial artists eventually died out, but it inspired many similar secret societies, especially martial arts clans.

Mo Zi's philosophy and system was just one of many forms of thought developing in China during the Spring and Autumn and Warring States periods. As a whole, they are called the "Hundred Schools". Their teachings covered politics, society, culture, morality, military strategy, and even mathematics.

Some schools were closely related. The School of Yin and Yang believed that the forces of yin (dark, feminine, and earthly) and yang (light, masculine, and heavenly) together made up everything in the universe. This later became the central principle of Taoism.

The Hundred Schools was a unique phenomenon in Chinese history, when political leaders and nobles were more open-minded and were willing to listen to all kinds of scholarly opinions.

14
Sun Zi and Sun Bin
The Art of War

"Therefore, a wise ruler is cautious and a good general is alert. This is the Way for keeping the nation at peace and the army whole."

Sun Bin wept as he bade farewell to his sworn brother, Pang Juan. From a tender age, the two of them had learnt military tactics and strategy from an old hermit in the mountains. Now Pang was setting off to make his career in the state of Wei, one of the seven major powers in China's Warring States Period.

Pang promised that if he became successful in Wei, he would call for Sun Bin to join him there as his comrade. He proclaimed, "If I don't keep my vow, let me be killed by a thousand arrows!"

Pang was hired by the Wei military, and he soon made his name as a brilliant general. Every battle he fought was a battle he won. It would soon be time to call for his friend Sun Bin.

Meanwhile, Sun Bin remained with their teacher, the mysterious Guigu Zi. Seeing that Pang had left, Guigu Zi revealed one of his most prized possessions: the 13 chapters of "The Art of War", a book by Sun Wu.

Sun Wu, respectfully known as Sun Zi, is perhaps the most famous strategist in history. He commanded armies in the wars among the states of Chu, Wu, and Yue before retiring to the mountains.

The knowledge contained in "The Art of War" is over 2,500 years old and was written with spears and swords in mind. Today, even though wars are fought with pilotless aircraft and cyberattacks, Sun Zi's wisdom remains required reading for military officers around the world.

But the bamboo strips containing "The Art of War" that Sun Bin had was the only copy of the book left. The others had all been lost when soldiers from the state of Yue set fire to the capital of Wu, burning down its library and many other treasures.

In the beginning of "The Art of War", Sun Zi said: "Warfare is an important matter for a nation. It is a matter of life and death, the way to survival or to destruction. It must be studied."

Legend has it that Sun Bin was Sun Zi's grandson. But this was not the reason Guigu Zi passed down the valuable teachings to him.

The Art of War, Guigu Zi told his student, could be used for good or evil. It was because he thought Sun Bin was a man of moral character that he was worthy.

Sun Bin learned the book by heart. Then, sure enough, his friend Pang recommended him to the king of Wei. Sun Bin soon received a letter from the Wei government summoning him for military service.

When Sun Bin was packing his things for the journey, Guigu Zi asked him to pick a flower for him. Sun Bin reached for a chrysanthemum standing in a bronze vase on his desk and held it up.

"Teacher, please use this flower to tell my fortune," said Sun Bin, putting the flower back in the vase.

Guigu Zi said: "This flower's stem is broken, so that's a bad sign. But the chrysanthemum is a flower that can withstand the winter cold. Even in bad conditions, it does not fall."

"Also," he continued, "the flower came from a bronze vase, and you returned it to its vase. This means that you will not carve out a career for yourself in Wei, but in your home country."

Sun Bin was from the state of Qi. Still, he bade his teacher farewell and travelled to Wei to join Pang, who had by now risen to become the overall commander of the Wei military.

Guigu Zi knew that his student would suffer great hardships. But this heavenly secret was not to be disclosed.

When Sun Bin arrived in Wei, he had a joyful reunion with his sworn brother. The king was also glad to have another disciple from Guigu Zi to serve him, and he wanted to make Sun Bin second-in-command of the army.

Pang objected. How could his sworn brother take a lower position than himself? It'd be fair to make Sun Bin an advisor and give him real power over the army once he achieved glory in combat. "Then I will give up my position to him," Pang declared.

They were beautiful words, but behind them was poisonous treachery. At Pang's insistence, Sun Bin became an advisor, someone who was welcome to speak but not to act. This was intentional; all the power remained in Pang's hands.

When Pang sat down to discuss military strategy with Sun Bin over a meal, he soon realized just how far behind he was lagging in knowledge compared with his classmate. He became curious and asked Sun Bin where he had learned his advanced methods.

Sun was not on his guard. He unwittingly told Pang how Guigu Zi had passed to him the secret book "The Art of War", written by his grandfather. Pang's curiosity darkened into intense jealousy.

Pang fabricated a story and said: "At the time, our master also taught me the same thing, but I didn't apply it myself and forgot the principles. Would you mind writing down the text for me so I can study them again?"

Sun Bin agreed and began writing down "The Art of War" word for word from memory.

Meanwhile, Pang was busy thinking of a plan to ruin Sun Bin so badly that he would never be able to rise above Pang and gain the favor of the king.

Pang forged a letter in Sun Bin's handwriting, which read that while Sun was serving the state of Wei, his true loyalty lay with his homeland of Qi. Pang immediately delivered this fake letter to the king of Wei.

The furious king told Sun Bin: "I've been so good to you, but all day long you have only the state of Qi on your mind." He prepared to have Sun Bin executed.

Pang needed his former classmate to write out "The Art of War", so he said to the king, "Death is too light a punishment for this rogue. Why don't we break his knees and tattoo the word 'treason' on his face so that he can never serve any state again?"

But when Pang met with Sun Bin, he pretended to be on

Sun Bin's side. Pang said: "The king wanted to kill you, but as your sworn brother I stepped in and begged him for mercy. Unfortunately, the laws of Wei mean that you have to be punished."

The unsuspecting Sun Bin thanked Pang and prepared to face his cruel punishment. "The flower I picked for my teacher back then had a broken stem," he remembered. "Now I am to have my kneecaps broken for a crime I didn't commit. Fate is unavoidable."

After the punishment was carried out, Pang provided Sun Bin with good food and comfortable lodging as he recuperated. Sun Bin slowly wrote out "The Art of War" for his friend. He could only complete about two or three bamboo strips per day.

About a month later, Pang became impatient. "At this rate, will I ever obtain the secret arts?" he complained to the servant looking after Sun Bin.

The servant thought Pang's attitude was strange, considering Sun Bin was supposed to be his sworn brother. He asked one of Pang's subordinates and learned that once Sun Bin finished writing out "The Art of War", Pang would have him killed. The servant was horrified at this betrayal and informed Sun Bin promptly.

Surrounded by enemies and unable to walk, Sun Bin struggled to find a way out. He recalled that Guigu Zi had given him a small pouch, which was to be opened only in an emergency. Sun Bin opened it and found the words: "PRETEND TO BE INSANE."

Sun Bin acted immediately. He began speaking gibberish and shoved all his completed work into the fireplace. Pang was at a loss. He tried cruel and unusual ways of getting Sun Bin to regain his sanity, but none worked. Finally, Sun Bin was left to rot in a pigsty. He pretended to enjoy the filth, and everyone was convinced he was a lost cause.

A couple of days later, Sun Bin managed to find an opportunity to escape and return to Qi just as Guigu Zi predicted. He became a secret advisor, helping General Tian Ji fight his battles.

Soon the states of Wei and Qi were at war.

In the course of battle, Pang found himself outclassed and outmatched, routed constantly, with troops destroyed and stratagems thwarted. Soon he began to suspect that Sun Bin was active in the enemy ranks. His suspicion turned to horror when, during one battle, the Qi troops raised a new set of battle flags with Sun Bin's name written on them.

Finally, Pang led his army to directly attack Sun Bin's forces. Pretending to retreat, Sun Bin used a masterful strategy: he had his men light fewer fires each night for cooking, tricking the enemy scouts into thinking that the Qi troops were deserting in large numbers. Pang was convinced that the mighty Qi army had shrunk to just a third of its original size.

The decisive blow came at Maling Pass, where Sun Bin's forces had marched. Along the way, in order to impede movement, they had cut down all the trees except one.

When Pang arrived with his men, it was nighttime. The Wei general saw the lone tree, gave an order for the path to be cleared, and waved a torch over the words: "Pang Juan dies under this tree."

Pang's torch fire created a target for thousands of Sun Bin's archers, and thousands of arrows flew forth. The Wei troops were slaughtered. As the battle ended, Sun Bin approached the wounded Pang.

Unrepentant, Pang said: "I regret not killing you when I made you a cripple. Now you've gained all the glory."

Consumed by jealousy, he drew his sword and took his own life.

The state of Wei lost its best general. Formerly one of the most powerful states in China, it began slipping into decline.

Sun Bin did not harbor hatred for Pang despite the betrayal. He set free Pang's nephew, who had been taken prisoner. Then he retired and, like his grandfather before him, went to live in the mountains.

15
Qu Yuan
When wise words fell on deaf ears

One day in the early 200s BC, an aging man in white robes wandered along the bank of a river. His brow was furrowed in anger, sadness, and regret. He had lost weight; his face, once energetic, was now gaunt and sallow. The sad figure came across a fisherman, who recognized him immediately.

"Are you not His Excellency the Minister?" the fisherman asked. "What brings you here?"

"This world is filthy; I alone am clean. Everyone is drunk, only I'm clear-headed. So I was fired," said the old man.

The fisherman replied: "If the world is so dirty, why not

just leap in and make it clean? If all others are drunk, why not drink with them and help them learn to control themselves?"

"Is it not so," the former minister replied, "that someone who has just bathed will desire his clothes and hat to be clean as well? How could he allow his pure body to be made dirty again? I would rather die in this stream and end up in the bellies of the fish, than be corrupted by the filth of this world."

The fisherman laughed and paddled away, but for Qu Yuan, the minister and poet who had recently been dismissed, and for the state of Chu, the kingdom he had served with all his heart, it was really no laughing matter at all.

Qu Yuan was born to a noble family in the year 340 BC in the state of Chu in southern China. An intense patriot and a high-ranking official, Qu was in charge of maintaining the ancestral temples and holding religious ceremonies. He was also responsible for educating the children of the nobility.

Chu, located around the great Yangtze River valley, was one of the seven major states of China. Though it was a half-civilized, half-barbarian land, the size and strength of Chu were considerable. At one point, it occupied over one million square kilometers, making it the biggest state on earth.

Among the seven states, Qin was becoming the most powerful, since its new king carried out the policies of Legalism and was turning his state into an economic and military superpower.

Other leaders were so alarmed by the progress of Qin that scholars in the rest of China established entire fields of learning in order to find ways to deal with Qin. These were known as the Schools of Vertical and Horizontal Alliances.

But instead of increasing cooperation between the states, the scholars crafted beautiful but dishonest arguments to make their own ideas seem more attractive than others'. Some of the "scholars" were in fact spies from Qin working to lead the six states against one another.

Using crafty diplomatic tricks, a travelling scholar paid by the Qin government successfully convinced King Huai of Chu to make enemies with the powerful state of Qi.

Qu Yuan could do nothing but watch as the king of his beloved state made mistake after mistake under the influence of the fraudulent scholar. Qu Yuan pleaded with King Huai to make an alliance with Qi against Qin, but he did not listen.

Apart from Qu Yuan, nobody in the Chu government seemed to care. Most of the high officials and members of the royal family simply passed their days living lives of luxury, pretending to be unaware of what was happening. They were annoyed with Qu Yuan's complaints.

Finally, a group of dishonest court officials told King Huai lies about Qu Yuan. The king believed them and sent Qu Yuan into exile. As if to further torture him, he was given his job back by King Huai's successor, only to be fired again, this time for good.

Wandering about his homeland, Qu Yuan pondered deeply the situation of his state and the ways of the world.

In his torment, Qu Yuan composed some of the earliest masterpieces of Chinese poetry. His long, thoughtful verses have been compared with the 19th century European Romantic style.

I adapted my life to the ancient way,

and refused the manners of the present day.
I won't conform to the modern age,
for I follow the path of a bygone sage.

In the year 278 BC, Qin general Bai Qi led an army that conquered Chu's capital, Yingdu.

There was no hope left. For Qu Yuan, the years in exile were enough. He weighed his robes with rocks, waded into the depths of the Miluo River, and drowned.

For the sake of righteousness, I die alone,
as the ancient sages would have done.

The great poet and loyal minister lost his reputation, his life, and his country, but today his name is immortal. When the villagers of his homeland heard that Qu Yuan had gone, they frantically boarded small, fast canoes—dragon boats—to find his body. When this failed, they bundled rice in leafy packaging and sank it into the depths of the river, hoping that the fish would be distracted away from eating his remains. The bundled rice is called "Zongzi" (sticky rice dumplings). The day Qu Yuan sacrificed his life became the Dragon Boat Festival, celebrated in memory of him.

Greatly weakened, the state of Chu lasted for another 50 years after Qu Yuan's death, until it was conquered by the king Ying Zheng of Qin in 224 BC. All other states fell too, and Ying Zheng became the First Emperor of the Qin Dynasty.

16
Shang Yang
Equal before the law

oday, we might think of government regulations and standards as a natural part of civilized life. In ancient times, however, many rulers relied only on the faith of their subjects and the power of their armies.

One of the main Chinese philosophies to rise in the Warring States Period was called Legalism. Its main objective, to introduce a system where the law stood above all men, was an all-new concept. But once it appeared, it would influence Chinese government and management for over 2,000 years.

One bright day in the mid-300s BC, a crowd gathered at the southern entrance of Xianyang, the capital of the state of Qin. There was a commotion in the marketplace as an official accompanied by several soldiers brought a small log and put it upright on the ground.

The official announced, "Whoever can move this wood log to the north entrance will be rewarded with 30 catties of gold." To be exact, "gold" at that time referred to copper, yet copper was also very expensive. The value was more than an average person could earn in a lifetime.

The people in the crowd could not believe their ears. Who in their right mind would give such a massive reward for this simple task? The log was not heavy; at most it would take half an hour for a man walking at a comfortable speed to finish the job. It had to be some kind of joke. The crowd was silent.

Since no one stepped forth, the official raised the reward to 50 catties.

Finally, a poor worker came forward to accept the task. "I'm just selling my physical labor every day, so I'm not losing much even if he doesn't pay me," he said. He picked up the log and walked northward, followed by the official, soldiers, and a large crowd of amused onlookers.

Half an hour later, the man set down the log in the center of the market at the northern gate of Xianyang. To everyone's surprise, the official indeed took out 50 catties of gold and handed it to the poor laborer.

"You are a good subject," the official said. "Take your reward. The government has made a promise, so we must keep our word."

This official was the reformer Shang Yang, and the ridiculously simple task he had just paid such a massive reward for was the first thing he did as the new minister of Qin.

Of course, Shang Yang's intention was not to have a log moved across town. His aim was to show the common people that the government would keep its word at all times.

Thanks to Shang Yang, the state of Qin was the first to seriously apply Legalist ideas.

Shang Yang was not born in Qin. He was a descendant of a noble in the small state of Wey (衛) who moved to the neighboring state of Wei (魏). Because of his family connections, he was able to become a secretary for a powerful senior minister in Wei. But the minister soon died and Shang Yang was not promoted.

In 361 BC, Duke Xiao of Qin came to the throne. He sent messengers to spread the word across all of China that he was looking for capable men to help him make Qin a great nation.

At the time, the state of Qin was known more for the quality of its horses and the beauty of its princesses, not cultural or political importance. It lay west of the Yellow River, forming a borderland between the heartland of Chinese civilization and the desert nomads of central Asia. Few would guess that it would one day not only dominate the country, but even inspire the name of "China" itself.

Shang Yang received the message, quit his job, and went to Qin.

He was granted an audience with Duke Xiao. To make sure Duke Xiao would listen to his ideas, Shang Yang spent three days droning on about the old ways of governance. The duke was bored and fell asleep several times.

Only on the fourth day did Shang Yang ask Duke Xiao what he was trying to achieve.

The Qin ruler's first and foremost

wish was to strengthen the military of the state. Shang Yang proposed a fitting solution, and injected energy into his voice to make sure the duke would listen. People in the world are basically selfish, he said. Without strict laws, everyone just looks out for their own interests and a strong group body cannot be formed. Yet, people are also greedy and afraid of death. Therefore, to govern a country, the ruler needs to provide handsome rewards for following orders and harsh punishments for breaking the law.

All of the above, Shang told Duke Xiao of Qin, meant that the authorities had to enforce a complete code of law. Only by the principles of Legalism could the government gain absolute trust and obedience from the ordinary people.

This time, Duke Xiao was wide awake and all ears. He had found the man he was looking for.

Shang Yang became chief adviser of Qin. To test out his new authority, he carried out a survey asking people what they thought about his publicity stunt with the laborer who was given 50 catties of gold to carry a log.

There were all kinds of opinions. Some thought the idea was a waste of money, and criticized Shang Yang for his foolishness. Others praised him.

But Shang Yang said: "Those who disagree with the policy should be punished for opposing the state. Those who praised it are just trying to gain favor with me, so they should also be punished."

The point of Legalism was to make people obey, not think. Duke Xiao was quite pleased and he let Shang Yang implement his laws throughout Qin.

Under Shang Yang, citizens of Qin were divided into 18 ranks. One could advance in rank by making public contributions. Shang also took land from the nobles and distributed it to ordinary peasants, who then became free to work the fields for themselves. Every five households formed an official unit with mutual interests, since the whole group would be held responsible if someone broke the law. The army had a similar system, with the sons of five families forming a military unit.

Even everyday customs were regulated by the government. Different generations in a family could not sleep on the same bed, which was typical for the poor, and people's personal lives were adjusted by law to encourage them to produce more children. In battle, a soldier who fought fearlessly and killed multiple enemy troops would boost his family's ranking; those who showed cowardice or retreated would have wrath brought upon their entire social unit.

The law meticulously detailed taxation, agricultural production, duties in marriage and to one's parents, military law, public order, and labor. Training centers and departments for inspection and execution were set up to ensure that everyone was on the same page.

Shang Yang paid particular attention to military equipment. Weapons were created according to specific standards and the names of the manufacturers were carved onto the arms to hold them responsible. The state of Qin also drew technological talent from other ethnic groups to help specialize and unify production. The crossbow and swords that Qin created during this time were of such high quality that even the Ming and Qing Dynasties 2000 years later were unable to match.

After a decade of reform, Qin built up a massive income that it used to strengthen its military across the entire people. The people of Qin State were already fierce fighters, but the reforms turned them into "legions of tigers and wolves", unstoppable in combat. Shang Yang led these armies to victory in multiple battles against the powerful Wei in central China. Qin absorbed new territory and fortresses into its land.

But Shang Yang's rules were cruel. People were encouraged to spy on each other and report on their neighbors and relatives if they broke the law. Even small violations were punished very severely, and the people of Qin lived in fear and loneliness.

Many nobles spoke out against the harsh minister that Duke Xiao had brought in. Part of the reason was that even as nobles, they too had to follow the laws that Shang Yang set. For example, the tutors of the duke's son acted unlawfully and were given humiliating sentences. One had words tattooed on his face to mark him as a criminal, and the other simply had his nose cut off.

Hundreds of nobles who disagreed with the laws were led to a gorge and killed. The river flowing below ran red and the screams of the dying could be heard for miles.

Qin was on the rise. It had taken important territory around the Yellow River that belonged to the mighty Wei State. Shang Yang was given his own territory within Qin and enjoyed a hero's life.

One day, Shang Yang was at a feast with many of his followers. He celebrated his victories, saying, "Look how successful I've become. I am like Baili Xi, wouldn't you say?"

Baili Xi was another well-known official of Qin State from about 300 years earlier. Before he had left home to find work, he had been so poor that his wife slaughtered their only chicken to give him a filling meal. After decades of hard work and patience, Baili Xi was so loved by the people of Qin that they wept for days after his death, as if their own fathers had died.

At this moment, a scholar at the feast stood up: "If you promise not to kill me, then I will say a few words" he said to Shang Yang, who granted this request.

"You know that you do not have the hearts of the people," he said. "When you go out, you are protected by the strongest of warriors as your bodyguards, always with blades at the ready. Otherwise you would never dare leave your residence. How can you be compared to Baili Xi?"

The scholar warned Shang Yang that his days of fortune would come to an end soon. His only way to avoid a sorry fate was to leave politics at once and give up his private territory.

Shang Yang did not have the scholar punished. However, he didn't listen to his advice either. But the words were absolutely correct.

Not just the ordinary people but also most of the nobles and even Duke Xiao's son disliked Shang Yang. They just did not show their displeasure because they feared punishment.

Once Duke Xiao died, his son rose to the throne and became King Huiwen. The new ruler remembered how Shang Yang had ruthlessly punished his teachers. He also knew how much others hated this man.

Very soon rumors began to spread that Shang Yang was

scheming to betray the king and start a rebellion. Shang Yang fled to his own territory, which just made him seem even more suspicious.

Finally, Shang Yang tried to flee back to Wei State. Along the way, he begged local folk on the road to the border to let him rest in their homes. But under the laws that he himself had created, even travel required official documents to certify government permission. Shang Yang had no such papers, so no one would open their doors to him.

Alone and terrified, Shang Yang was arrested by Qin soldiers. He was sentenced to death for treason and killed by a torture method that he himself had invented. Five ropes were tied to his arms, legs, and neck, and the ends were fastened to five horse-drawn chariots. The chariots were driven off in five different directions at once, and Shang Yang was torn to pieces.

Shang Yang was dead, but the laws he created were so effective that King Huiwen and all the Qin kings after him continued to use his system. Qin State grew more powerful and expanded in all directions. The six other states of China looked on with fear and readied their own defenses. They fought many wars against Qin, but none would prevail.

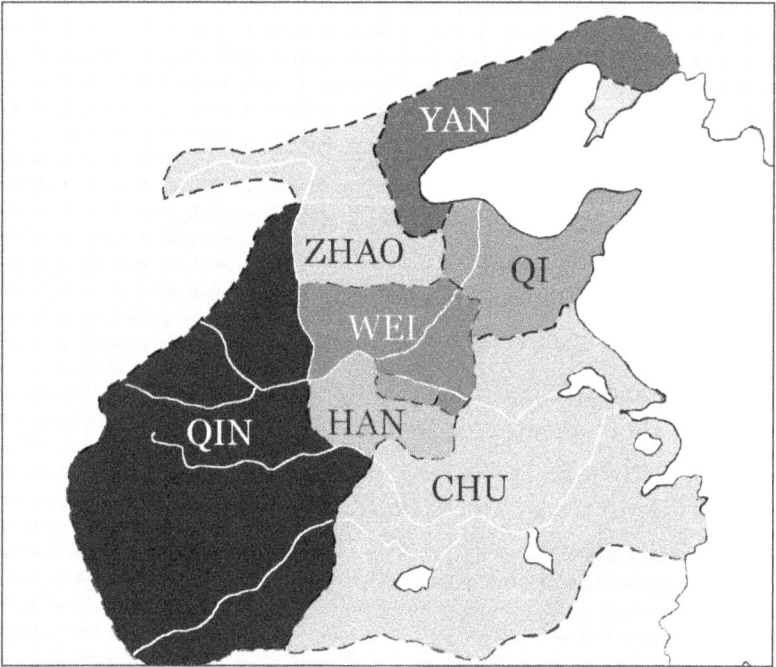

The Warring States Period engulfed the last 250 years of the Zhou Dynasty. Seven major states fought against each other. Ultimately Qin State would prevail.

17
Ying Zheng
King of Qin

The Warring States Period from around 475 to 221 BC was a time of bitter and desperate fighting. Each of the seven major states was determined to achieve complete dominance in China.

For over a hundred years, the powerful states of Qin and Zhao had fought countless battles. In 260 BC, Zhao was defeated in the Battle of Changping. Qin's brilliant but ruthless general Bai Qi lured 400,000 Zhao soldiers into a massive trap and killed their leader. With no way out, the Zhao army surrendered. Bai Qi showed no mercy and had all of the survivors buried alive.

A year later, the boy destined to become the First Emperor of China was born. He did not grow up in a palace, and few of his Qin countrymen knew of his existence. In fact, he was not even born in the state of Qin, and his mother was not from Qin either. She was a native of Zhao, and her son grew up living among enemies.

The birth of Ying Zheng, future King of Qin, began as a business investment.

At the time of the Battle of Changping, a wealthy merchant named Lü Buwei was travelling through the state of Zhao. In Handan, the capital, he met a Qin man named Yiren.

Yiren was a Qin prince, but not a very important one.

Trading royal family members around was common diplomacy among the seven states, and Yiren was one of those unlucky enough to have been chosen for this role. But Lü Buwei saw an opportunity to turn the prince into an asset. He befriended Yiren and let him marry one of his concubines, a beauty known only as Lady Zhao. She soon gave birth to a son, Ying Zheng.

Because of where he was born, Ying Zheng was actually called Zhao Zheng in his childhood. Growing up in Handan, the capital of Zhao, he was surrounded by enemies. His only friends were the children of other foreign royals living in Handan, and even then, they were not true friends. Prince Dan of Yan State, who spent his childhood with Ying Zheng, would later try to have him killed.

When Lü Buwei got the chance, he smuggled Yiren out of Zhao. That was just the first step. Using his money and connections, Lü Buwei placed Yiren on the Qin throne. Lady Zhao became the queen, and Lü gave himself a powerful position: Chancellor of Qin.

At the age of eight, Zhao Zheng was finally allowed to leave Zhao and see his true homeland. His name was changed to Ying Zheng.

In the year 247 BC, Yiren died. Ying Zheng was just 13 when he became King of Qin.

For twelve years, Ying Zheng had no authority. Lü Buwei controlled the government and Queen Zhao was the most powerful person in the royal palace. She and her secret lover Lao Ai had two sons and they plotted to dethrone Ying Zheng.

The king was completely alone. But he stayed calm, like a

tiger in its mountain. Soon it would be time to show everyone to whom the kingdom truly belonged.

Time flew. Proud of the children Queen Zhao had with him, Lao Ai began to act as though he himself was a royal. Having many admirers and the beautiful queen by his side made him cocky. He bragged at a drunken party about being the king's stepfather. Rumors began to spread and Lao Ai thought that maybe one of his sons could be king too.

Even then, the king made no move. Lao Ai thought the throne was in his grasp. One day, he gathered hundreds of his followers in Xianyang, Qin's capital. They armed themselves and tried to take the palace by force.

But it was Ying Zheng, not Lao Ai, who would seize power that day. As Lao Ai's men moved to attack, thousands of battle-hardened Qin soldiers stepped out to meet them. Shocked by the king's sudden strike, Lao Ai turned tail and ran away. The blood of his slaughtered men spilled on the palace grounds.

Ying Zheng ordered a massive search for Lao Ai and those connected to him, and he brought them to justice. He punished his treacherous mother Queen Zhao by imprisoning her for life. The two illegitimate sons she had with Lao Ai were found, thrown into bags, and beaten to death. And Lao Ai was caught and sentenced to be torn apart by chariots.

The year Ying Zheng defeated Lao Ai and seized power was 235 BC. He was about 25 years old.

To the Chinese of 2,200 years ago, the seven states with their own cultures and customs made up the entire world. They called this *tian xia*, or "all under heaven." Uniting China —the dream of Ying Zheng and the kings before him—would be like trying to take over all of Earth today.

One day, Lü Buwei received a guest from the state of Chu. The visitor was a scholar named Li Si. Unable to find a government position in his own country, he went to Qin. Soon, Li Si was granted a meeting with the king himself.

Like Shang Yang a century before him, Li Si impressed Ying Zheng with his bold ideas. Qin was the most powerful nation in China, but it had no hope of defeating the other six states if they formed an alliance.

On the other hand, if Qin could attract foreign scholars and other talented people to work for it, it would be able to outsmart the enemy nations. If these individuals could not be convinced to join Qin, they should be assassinated, Li Si said.

Some officials disapproved of it, because they did not want to see too many foreigners in Qin. Li Si wrote a long letter to counter their arguments. Eventually, Li Si became an important official under the king and came up with many strategies to help Ying Zheng conquer the rest of China.

Five years later, Qin attacked and conquered Han, the smallest of the six states. The final war had begun.

The state of Zhao had a long and glorious history. It was home to a proud people. Even after losing 400,000 men in the Battle of Changping, the Zhao army was prepared to fight to the end.

The end came in 228 BC. Qin commander Wang Jian led a massive and well-trained force to overwhelm the Zhao defences. No other state stepped in to help. The capital city of Handan was captured and the state of Zhao ceased to exist.

Qin struck greater fear into the hearts of the other leaders.

One of these leaders was Prince Dan of the state of Yan, the man who had spent his childhood in Zhao with Ying Zheng. But their friendship was long over. The fall of Zhao turned the states of Yan and Qin into neighbors. They were not yet at war, but peace was dying. Prince Dan decided that the only thing he could do to save his state was to have Ying Zheng killed.

One night, Prince Dan received a visitor from Qin. It was General Fan Wuji. He had run away from Qin and the government had killed his entire family as punishment. Day and night he thought about ways to avenge his relatives.

Next to arrive was the legendary Jing Ke. Jing Ke was from the state of Wei, which was already at war with Qin. He was a skilled swordsman and poet. His homeland was being occupied, and Prince Dan accepted him with open arms.

Jing Ke volunteered to go to the capital of Qin, to kill Ying Zheng. To get permission from the Qin authorities to see the king as an envoy, he needed a good reason.

General Fan was a man with a price on his head in the state of Qin. If Jing Ke brought his head to Qin, he might be able to see the king. Hearing this, General Fan drew his sword and killed himself.

Armed with the general's head, Jing Ke was ready to begin his mission. To please the Qin kingdom even more, Prince Dan prepared a map showing large and fertile western territories belonging to the state of Yan. Jing Ke would unroll the map while saying that these lands were to be given to Qin in exchange for peace. But hidden in the map was Jing Ke's weapon—a sharp, poisoned dagger.

It was a cold winter day when Jing Ke crossed the Yi River to go west to Qin. Clad in the white robes of mourning, Prince Dan and his companions watched him go. They knew that even if Jing Ke accomplished his mission, he would be captured and killed.

As Jing Ke left, he sang.
"The wind is howling, the waters of the Yi River are freezing. The hero is gone, he will not return."

Jing Ke gained entry to the imperial court of Qin in Xianyang. He ascended the steps to the throne, carrying the map in one hand and the box containing General Fan's head in the other.

As Jing Ke carefully unrolled the map, Ying Zheng looked eagerly at the drawings of the towns, rivers, and farmland on it. He would get these lands without losing a single man.

Then the map reached its end, revealing the dagger within. Jing Ke seized it and lunged at the Qin king, grabbing his long, flowing silk robes in the hope of ensuring a hit. The terrified king pulled back, and his sleeves ripped. Jing Ke missed. He lunged again, but Ying Zheng had gotten up and run.

Everyone in the imperial court stood in deathly silence around the platform where Ying Zheng's throne stood. By order of the strict laws of Qi, under no circumstances could anybody enter without direct permission from the king. But Ying Zheng was too frightened to even scream, let alone issue orders.

Finally, a royal doctor threw his medicine bag at the assassin. Jing Ke was startled, for a second, he lost sight of his victim. Then a guard cried at Ying Zheng to draw his sword. Doing as he was told, the king turned to face his would-be-killer. Jing Ke had one final chance. He aimed, and threw his dagger at Ying Zheng.

The blade missed. Jing Ke chuckled and accepted defeat.

Overcome with shock, Ying Zheng raised his own blade and struck Jing Ke again and again. After stabbing Jing Ke eight times, the king turned to his court and let out a tortured cry. No one had dared help him in his moment of most terrible danger. Even with so much power, he was still alone.

There are many famous assassins in Chinese history who gave their lives for the sake of their lords or states. Jing Ke is probably the greatest of them. His tragic failure marked the end of all hope for the remaining four states in the war against Qin.

Ying Zheng's armies swept across China. Jing Ke's homeland of Wei fell. Almost all males fit for military service in Qin were mobilized to form a horde that rapidly brought the great Chu kingdom to its knees. The king of Yan, father of Prince Dan, killed his son in a desperate attempt to apologize to Qin for the assassination attempt. Ying Zheng ignored his pleas and Yan was vanquished without remorse. Standing alone, the once-powerful state of Qi surrendered without a fight.

It was the year 221 BC. Ying Zheng was now Qin Shi Huang—the First Emperor of Qin Dynasty and the First Emperor of China. Qin Dynasty was the fourth dynasty in Chinese history. For the first time in history, China was truly united.

18
Qin Shi Huang
The First Emperor

The First Emperor, *Qin Shi Huang*, is so important that the English name for China comes from his name.

When King Ying Zheng of Qin conquered the other six states, China had been in chaos for over 500 years. By 221 BC, he had got rid of those who opposed him in his own government, survived a cunning attempt on his life by the assassin Jing Ke, and led his generals to absolute victory, ending the Warring States Period.

Because the "q" in "Qin" is pronounced "ch," it is not surprising to see that the English word "China" comes from the Qin Dynasty.

Ying Zheng was the first Chinese leader to call himself *huang di* (皇帝), which is translated as "emperor." Before that, only the ancient rulers of legendary times, like the Yellow Emperor, or Yao, Shun, and Yu, had called themselves *di* (帝). Other ancient rulers were sometimes called *huang* (皇). But that was over two thousand years before Qin's day. By the time of unification, the terms *huang* and *di* were so honorable that people associated them with gods.

By calling himself *Qin Shi Huang Di* (秦始皇帝), or the First Emperor of the Qin Dynasty, Ying Zheng intended to create a faith among his people that had never existed before.

The Qin Dynasty lasted only 12 years. But what the First Emperor accomplished during his time on the throne changed China forever.

Qin Shi Huang was a strong and ruthless leader. Hundreds of years before he was born, the state of Qin had started practicing Legalism, which meant that the law of the king was absolute. The society and army of Qin became powerful and unified China. The conquering would continue.

In the north, Qin Shi Huang sent a 300,000-strong army under the command of General Meng Tian to attack the nomadic barbarians that often raided Chinese lands. Once they were punished, walls were built to keep them out. The walls were made of wood, but subsequent emperors would improve on them to create the majestic Great Wall we know today.

In the south, beyond the land of Chu, were the Bai Yue or Hundred Yue peoples. Qin Shi Huang sent an army of 500,000 men to invade the Yue lands and settled Chinese there. Tropical diseases and unfavorable conditions stopped the first invasion, but Qin Shi Huang did not give up. Qin workers dug the massive Lingqu Canal to allow ships to sail between north and south China. Supplies and people began to flow, and the south was conquered eventually. The current provinces of Fujian, Guangdong, Guangxi, and even what is now northern Vietnam were made part of the Qin empire.

At the same time, Qin Shi Huang knew that his people needed to live in peace. Instead of killing or removing the kings and nobles of the states he conquered, he ordered them to move to the imperial capital of Xianyang so that they would be under the direct control and protection of the imperial government. He also ordered that all weapons not in the hands of his soldiers be melted down and turned into tools.

As China was divided into many states for centuries, the

language and writing varied from place to place. This had to change for China to continue to be one unified country. Chinese characters were standardized, so that people could understand each other's writing in any part of the empire, no matter how different their spoken dialects were.

Today, China has hundreds of dialects, but the writing has only undergone minor changes since Qin Shi Huang's day. It is possible for a modern Chinese to understand ancient documents. This would be as though learning English gave you the ability to read other European languages, as well as ancient Greek and Latin.

Qin Shi Huang's Legalist minister Li Si warned that the influence of too many types of thinking would cause disunity among the recently-conquered peoples. Books that the government did not approve, such as those that recorded the history of the defeated states, were burned. But Qin Shi Huang respected the value of this knowledge, so copies were held in the imperial libraries. Only those with special permission could read them.

The emperor's son, Fu Su, was a scholar and spoke out against burning the books. As punishment, Qin Shi Huang sent him to the north to help General Meng Tian fight the nomads.

Even though the policies of Legalism were dictatorial and sometimes cruel, Qin Shi Huang decided he had to rule his people with the harshest methods or else China would split up again. His son Fu Su's interest in other philosophies, such as Confucianism, did not stop Qin Shi Huang from making him his chosen successor. It is possible the First Emperor did not intend his strict rule to be permanent.

Qin Shi Huang knew that his country needed to be connected. So he ordered the construction of major highways running in all directions to and from Xianyang. The roads were built with advanced techniques to facilitate the smooth transport of goods and deployment of armies between any part of the empire. The biggest roads had 50 lanes for horse carts.

Aside from standardizing the Chinese language, the Qin government also unified all forms of currency, weights, measurements, and even very specific standards such as the width of road lanes and the chariots driving on them. This brought about economic development.

The Qin government was also quite developed. Qin Shi Huang divided his administration into three branches: the executive, military, and legal branches. This is similar to the separation of powers described in the United States Constitution.

The Qin emperor was a well-disciplined and very spiritual man. He slept little and forced himself to read a certain number of official documents every day. To measure how much work he had completed, he had a special scale to put his finished books on. Once the weight of the books reached the required amount of reading for the day, a bell would ring and only then would the emperor take a rest.

For thousands of years, Chinese have believed in the will of heaven and that people have the ability to cultivate their minds and attain immortality. The First Emperor too wished not just to conquer the world but to reach greater spiritual realms.

In his five tours across the empire, Qin Shi Huang visited famous mountains and other landmarks to hold ceremonies respecting heaven and earth.

The First Emperor also believed in the Chinese Theory of the Five Elements that made up the universe—wood, fire, earth, metal, and water. According to the experts, the element of the Qin Dynasty was water. Its auspicious color was black, its direction north, and its number 6. To abide by these teachings and follow the flow of nature, Qin Shi Huang ordered the use of multiples of 6 wherever possible. For example, the width of a horse cart was 6 feet. The number of provinces in the empire was 36.

Qin Shi Huang sent many expeditions to look for the land of immortals, hoping that he would learn how to cultivate himself spiritually and perhaps even live forever as an immortal. None of these expeditions succeeded, but they may have discovered the islands of Taiwan and Japan and introduced Chinese culture to those places. One of the men the First Emperor sent to find the secret of eternal life was Xu Fu, who took 3,000 young boys and girls in his fleet. It is said that he landed in Japan and helped found the Japanese nation. Whether or not these legends are true, the Japanese did begin using Chinese writing and farming techniques around this time.

Even if he could not live forever, Qin Shi Huang wanted his empire to last for ten thousand years. The First Emperor's son Fu Su was a bright and talented man, and everyone expected him to take over the throne when Qin Shi Huang died.

The First Emperor's wish did not come true. After his death in 210 BC, imperial officials such as his minister Li Si and the wicked eunuch Zhao Gao betrayed him. They used his imperial pen to forge a letter saying that Qin Shi Huang had wanted his second son Huhai to be emperor, and forced crown prince Fu Su to commit suicide.

Huhai, known as Qin Er Shi or "Qin II," ascended to the throne, but he had little interest. This was perfect for the treacherous officials who wanted real power for themselves, but even they could not hold it for long. Three years later, rebellions broke out and Qin II was killed along with the officials who controlled him.

The Qin Dynasty lasted only for 12 years. Seven years of rebellion and civil war followed, and the Han Dynasty was founded on the foundations of the Qin Dynasty. Even though the First Emperor's dynasty was short, his wish for order and unity has never died out in the hearts of Chinese people.

As a writing carved into a rock during the First Emperor's reign says:

"The Emperor took pity on the people and sent his legions to end violence with the force of martial virtue. Evil was sentenced, righteous faith was used to guide the people, and mighty virtue was established. All have submitted to it, the violent and rebellious have been exterminated, and the people have been saved. The empire is at peace. Law has been established, the world is under proper governance. This order will last forever."

The Qin Dynasty not only unified China's territory but also made the Chinese people one nation by unifying its language and culture.

19
Liu Bang
Destined for greatness

Some time after the death of First Emperor, Qin Shi Huang, in 210 BC, a low-ranking officer called Liu Bang was escorting convicts to help construct the imperial mausoleum.

Along the way, Liu Bang noticed that his group was getting smaller and smaller—the prisoners were escaping! The laws of Qin were strict. He would certainly be held responsible for the deserters. What was the point of getting to his destination only to be punished?

Doing some simple math, Liu Bang stopped the march. After treating his prisoners to wine, he told them they were free to go. But it was the mighty Qin government they were up against. They decided to follow their new leader.

Liu Bang was the son of peasants, and with his tiny band his chances were slim. But he had what the Chinese call *tian ming*—the Mandate of Heaven to rule the land.

Liu Bang stood six feet tall and commanded attention. He had a habit of entering taverns and getting so caught up in conversations that he forgot to pay for his drinks. But no one seemed to mind, since he attracted large crowds of customers wherever he went.

Once, Liu Bang talked his way into a gathering meant for nobles. He met a wealthy man and his daughter, Lü Zhi. Skilled in the ways of oracles, she said that he possessed the *qi*, or spiritual energy, of a king. Pleased, her father gave Liu Bang her hand in marriage.

The death of the First Emperor was the beginning of the end for the Qin Dynasty. The treacherous eunuch Zhao Gao murdered the rightful successor to the throne and replaced him with a dissolute puppet. Zhao Gao's rule was harsh and senseless, giving rise to many rebellions. Rumor had it that the seven states of China would rise again.

By 209 BC, China was in turmoil. Peasant commanders Chen Sheng and Wu Guang disobeyed orders from the government to work on a northern construction project, and they formed their own army. Both men were soon killed, but the damage to Qin had been done.

The Xiang military family revived the mighty state of Chu and were prepared to do battle with the imperial army. Their general was Xiang Yu, a ruthless warrior whose power was unmatched. In eastern China, he created an

alliance with other rebels and destroyed a Qin army much larger than his own. The empire was falling apart.

Meanwhile, Liu Bang and his men fumbled through China. He was a poor commander. Each time they attacked a city, they were defeated and forced to regroup for a new target.

Then one day, a man appeared at Liu's camp. It was the scholar Li Yiji, and he wished to offer his advice.

Liu Bang scoffed. He was not keen on hearing this intellectual ramble on about theories and ideas he could not understand, and he was prepared to send Li Yiji away. But when the scholar said he wanted to drink the night away, Liu Bang decided they might be able to see eye to eye.

The city of Chenliu, Li Yiji said, held vast stocks of grain and valuable supplies. Li knew the magistrate of Chenliu, so he would be able to convince him to surrender to Liu Bang's army.

Li Yiji met with the magistrate, but the latter refused to give up the city to the rebels. Li Yiji returned that very night and killed him. The following morning, he held up the head of the official to the people of Chenliu, and they surrendered.

At this time, most Qin troops were in the east battling Xiang Yu's rebel forces. Xiang Yu had become the top general of the state of Chu, ruled by King Huai II.

To support the anti-Qin rebel cause, King Huai II issued a royal edict: the first general to enter the home territory of the state of Qin in the land of Guanzhong would become its ruler.

Their stomachs full of the grain captured in Chenliu, Liu Bang's army began a proud march west to Guanzhong.

Liu Bang conquered Xianyang, the imperial capital in Guanzhong, almost without a fight. Seeing the abundance of riches, fantastic architecture, beautiful women, and other marvels of imperial civilization, Liu Bang was ready to settle in and enjoy himself with his comrades.

But his loyal advisor and childhood friend, Xiao He, intervened. It was important to keep discipline, he warned Liu Bang. The Qin empire had fallen because of indulgent, greedy men. Liu Bang could not make the same mistakes.

Liu Bang listened. His army did not harm civilians, respected the law, and left the king of Qin in peace after removing him from the throne and giving him a job as local chancellor. Precious books and documents were moved out of the imperial palace and kept safe.

The Qin Dynasty was gone, but danger was on the horizon. Xiang Yu had emerged victorious in the east and was coming to claim greater victories. Though he was a subject of Chu, he had never really agreed with his king's order that the first general to enter Guanzhong would become its rightful ruler. Soon, Xiang Yu had King Huai II murdered and seized power for himself. He called himself Hegemon King of Western Chu and would not stop until all of China was in his hands.

Liu Bang and his comrades were in a bad position. To Xiang Yu, it seemed insulting that he was forced to do most of the fighting against Qin while Liu Bang enjoyed a smooth advance to the imperial capital.

When Liu Bang heard about Xiang Yu's anger, he greeted the Chu troops and expressed sincere apologies for getting there first. He told Xiang Yu that in fact he had only intended to keep the territory under control so that he could turn its riches over to the great Hegemon, and that he would cause no further trouble.

Xiang Yu accepted this explanation for the time being, and marched onto Xianyang.

Unlike Liu's forces, which maintained order and respected the people, the Chu soldiers killed people and looted cities and villages wherever they went. Xiang Yu had the retired Qin emperor murdered.

To top off the killing and destruction, Chu soldiers set the imperial palace and library of Epang on fire. The entire palace complex burned for three continuous months, causing a huge setback for ancient Chinese knowledge, culture, and technology.

Breaking King Huai II's promise, Xiang Yu instead made Liu Bang the king of Hanzhong, a small territory in the southwest.

Liu Bang's army was no match for Western Chu, so he decided to take his submission to Xiang Yu at the Feast of Hong Gate.

Xiang Yu's wise advisor Fan Zeng observed Liu and his men carefully at the feast. He warned Xiang Yu that though Liu was weak, he was certain to become a future threat. But Xiang Yu paid no attention to his warning. Fan Zeng was not the only one who feared Liu Bang. Xiang Yu's cousin, Xiang Zhuang, drew a sword and stepped out into the hall. He began a sword dance, aiming at Liu Bang as he performed. Liu and his comrades realized right away that they were in great danger. Liu Bang excused himself and left the banquet in a hurry.

A subordinate presented a gift of jade to Xiang Yu as an apology for Liu Bang's rudeness.

Seeing that Liu Bang had escaped, Fan Zeng grabbed the fine jade and threw it on the ground. He criticized Xiang Yu for not killing Liu Bang when he had the chance. "We will all become his prisoners!" he said.

In 206 BC, Liu Bang took his army to Hanzhong, the small territory that Xiang Yu had given him.

He soon became the archenemy of Xiang Yu the Hegemon King, the mightiest general in the land.

The Chu-Han Contention had begun. And with the help of a previously unknown commander, the noble and brilliant Han Xin, Liu Bang prevailed over Xiang Yu in the year 202 BC. He officially became emperor of the Han Dynasty, which was China's fifth major dynasty and lasted around 400 years.

20
Han Xin
Pillar of the Nation

arly on in the war between Chu and Han, 14 men in the Han army were convicted of breaking military law. The punishment was execution by beheading.

Most of the men wept or begged for their lives as the executioner sent them into the next world. Only one man remained calm: the 14th convict. He maintained a steely expression, until it was his turn to lose his head.

Just as the blade was about to fall, the prisoner shouted with such might that everyone froze.

"I thought our King wanted to rule all of China! Why would you kill the man who can help you?!"

Seeing the prisoner's noble look and noting his bravery, the general spared him. This man was Han Xin, a lowly soldier who would become none other than the greatest general under Liu Bang. He never lost a battle and in many cases scored miraculous victories when outnumbered by many times.

Han Xin came from a family of poor nobles. His father died early, so he had no connections to do business or become a government official. Everybody shunned this penniless and often jobless young man. But his steadfast and ambitious character gave him the strength he needed to achieve greatness.

When the Qin Dynasty fell, Han Xin joined Xiang Yu's

army, but defected to Liu Bang later when Xiang Yu ignored all his advice. In Liu Bang's army, he was just a cook or common sentry.

In 206 BC, Liu Bang was made king of the Hanzhong region in southwest China. As most of his soldiers were from the east, many of them became homesick and deserted. Han Xin was one of those who ran away.

One day, Liu Bang heard that even his best advisor and a good friend, Xiao He, had fled. Liu Bang was furious and desperate. If he could not even trust Xiao He to remain loyal, who else would still follow him?

But that night, Xiao He came back and brought Han Xin with him.

"Why did you desert?" Liu Bang said.

"I didn't desert," Xiao He said. "I went to find this man, who was deserting."

"Who on earth is he?"

"Han Xin."

"Of all the generals and officers who ran away, why did you go after this man? What's so special about him?"

Xiao He said, "My Lord, the others are average people. But Han Xin has no equal. If you have the ambition to break out of this land and rule all of China, he is the man you need."

Liu Bang was skeptical, but he trusted Xiao He. He agreed to make Han Xin a grand marshal, to make sure that he would serve no one else but the Han.

Han Xin's first mission was to retake Guanzhong. Earlier, Xiang Yu had forced Liu Bang to give up this strategic land

and retreat to the
remote Hanzhong
region, an area which
was surrounded by
steep mountains. It
was only accessible
via vertigo-inducing
plank roads, built
by carving holes
into the sides of cliffs
and inserting logs,
before placing beams
upon them to make the
walkways.

To trick Xiang Yu
into thinking that
he did not have any
intention to conquer
the rest of China,
Liu Bang destroyed
the plank roads.
Repairing
them would be
difficult and time-
consuming.

The time had
come for Liu Bang
to reveal his true colors, and
Han Xin needed a plan. But first he needed a way to move his
men to attack Guanzhong.

The enemy was surprised, and then amused to find that
Han Xin had sent several hundred laborers to rebuild the

plank walkways. At such pace, it would take years to finish the construction, and even then, the fragile and narrow plank roads could be easily blocked off by an army guarding at the end.

Seeing that the enemy army was gathered at the other end of the plank way, Han Xin and his main force took an alternate route, via the city of Chencang. Enemy commander Zhang Han was expecting an attack from the mountains, and was taken by complete surprise.

"Advancing through the hidden path of Chencang" is now a well-known Chinese saying. But it was in the battle of Jingxing that Han Xin secured his most famous and spectacular victory.

After Han Xin took Guanzhong, Liu Bang's Han empire could begin pushing north and east. Han Xin led the attack to the north, conquering five states with armies far larger than his own.

Han Xin's army was composed of just around 10,000 old or inexperienced troops. First he used stratagem to cross the Yellow River and conquer the states of Wei and Dai.

Next was the state of Zhao. In the Warring States Period, it was the main enemy of Qin and had fought nearly to the last man before it was conquered by the First Emperor. Now, it was no weak state either. The king was Zhao Xie and his top general was a man called Chen Yu. They had 200,000 men versus Han Xin's 10,000-strong army.

Chen Yu was no great strategist, but under him was a skilled officer called Li Zuoche. Li noticed two things. One, the troops of Han Xin must be extremely tired from prolonged marching. Two, in order to get through to attack

Zhao, the Han forces would have to cross a mountain chain by going through the pass at Jingxing. At its narrowest point, only one soldier and a horse could pass at a time. Stopping Han Xin and bringing his head back to the king was a simple matter of blocking one end of the pass, cutting off supply, and waiting a couple weeks, Li concluded.

This was a sound plan, and it should have worked. But Chen Yu believed that as a scholar, he should fight honorably, especially when he enjoyed such a huge numerical advantage. He cited Sun Zi's Art of War to back up his point: "When you outnumber the enemy ten to one, surround him."

"We outnumber Han Xin twenty to one," Chen Yu argued. "If we have to resort to strategy to win, won't that make us look like a bunch of weaklings?" He decided to face Han Xin's army in the field.

Han Xin stayed on top of things at all times. He had many spies and scouts who kept track of the movements of the Zhao army for him. As soon as Han Xin heard that Li Zuoche's strategy was rejected, he ordered all his 10,000 men to go through Jingxing Pass.

The operation had three phases: First, he separated 2,000 men from his main force and had them hold up the red flags of the Han. They made their way to a mountain and hid there.

Next, Han Xin told everyone, "it's morning now. We're going to attack the Zhao camp and have a grand feast there this afternoon." But not even Han Xin's officers had faith in their leader's optimism.

After breakfast, Han Xin ordered all troops to cross the Tao River and set up camps on the riverbank. Normally, this is regarded as a great mistake in military tactics since it cuts off any hope of retreat.

Then Han Xin held up his grand marshal's banner, and rode proudly out of Jingxing Pass. The Zhao troops, eager for a chance to capture his battle standard, turned their attention to him and ignored the main force.

Han Xin fought for a while, then retreated to his main camp by the Tao River. As Han Xin made his way over, he purposefully had his officers and generals drop their banners to the ground. The Zhao troops were attracted by these trophies and struggled to pick them up as proof of their valor in battle.

The bulk of the Zhao army clashed with the Han. The less than 10,000 defenders fought frantically, knowing the only other way out for them was to be drowned. While the two sides were locked in battle, Han Xin ordered the 2,000 men hiding in the mountain to charge forth around the masses of the enemy soldiers, and marched straight into empty base, which was left empty at the time. They took down all of the Zhao banners and replaced them with the red flags of Han.

When the Zhao troops marched back to their camp, they found that it had been captured. At this moment the Han soldiers made one final charge from both sides and routed the forces of Zhao. King Zhao Xie and his general Chen Yu were killed.

Explaining his tactics, Han Xin said, "I forced my men to fight their way out of desperation. So they prevailed." This is also a lesson from Sun Zi's Art of War.

Like the advance through Chencang, Han Xin's victory over Zhao became another well-known saying: *bei shui yi zhan*, or "fighting with one's back to the water."

Han Xin knew that his victory was largely a matter of good

luck. After the battle he immediately ordered his men to find the Zhao commander Li Zuoche, the general whose strategy was considered too intelligent for General Chen Yu's honor.

Li said, "In August you conquered Wei. In September you crushed Dai. Now you've defeated Zhao. Your main advantage now is your reputation as a great general."

Li Zuoche then warned Han Xin, "But you are low on grain and your men are tired." The next target, Yan, would be difficult to subdue quickly. So he advised Han Xin not to attack Yan. Rather, he should make use of his mighty records in battles to frighten its leaders into submission.

Indeed, Yan surrendered quickly. The conquest of the north took Han Xin just a year, and soon he was marching south to take Qi.

With control of Guanzhong, western China had come under Han control. Defeating Wei, Dai, Zhao, Yan, and Qi meant that Han Xin had singlehandedly conquered six of the seven states in the Warring States Period. This is an unparalleled feat. Western Chu—Xiang Yu's homeland—was the only major power left to oppose Liu Bang. Control of the empire was in sight.

Even in greatness, Han Xin did not forget those who had helped him. He found the woman who had given him food for a month while he was just a fisherman, and gave her 1,000 pieces of gold.

Later, Han Xin returned to find the ruffian who had once forced him to crawl between his legs. Seeing that a great general had come looking, the man fled, fearing for his life. But instead Han Xin said, "He's a brave man. I could have killed him easily back then if it wasn't for the law." He promoted the ruffian to become a local security official.

When Liu Bang emerged victorious in 202 BC and brought order to China, Han Xin was celebrated as a war hero of the Han Dynasty. But Liu Bang distrusted him because he wielded too much power, and Liu's scheming empress Lü Zhi hated him even more. She teamed up with Xiao He, Liu Bang's childhood friend to lure Han Xin into a trap. They accused him of treason and had him tortured to death. Because Xiao He was the man who had originally recommended Han Xin to Liu Bang, it is said that Han Xin owed both his life and death to him.

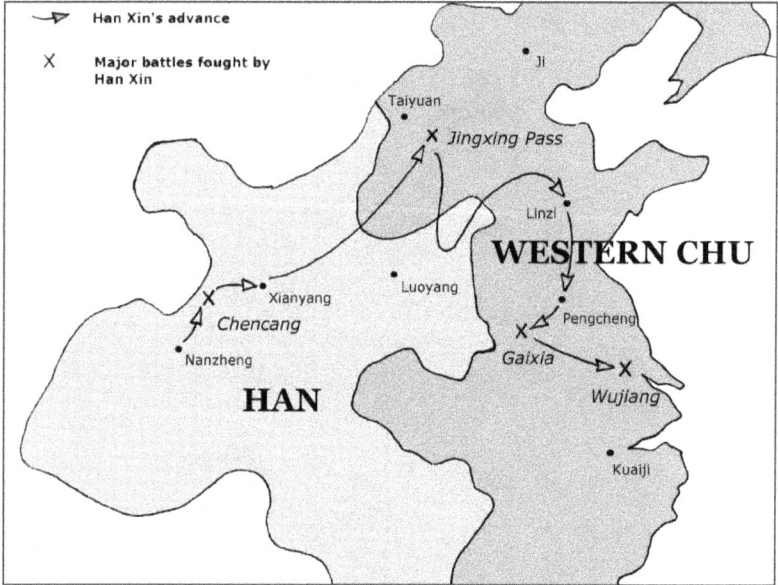

Starting out with a tiny army, General Han Xin (韓信) conquered northern China for Emperor Liu Bang, ensuring the victory of the Han (漢) Dynasty.

21
Xiang Yu
The Hegemon King

In the final years of Emperor Qin's reign, there was a man from the land of Chu called Xiang Liang. He had committed murder and was on the run with his nephew Xiang Yu.

Unexpectedly, the Xiangs sighted the emperor himself as he paraded through the land on one of his inspection tours.

"I could replace that man," the boy Xiang Yu told his uncle. "Don't say that! If someone hears you, our whole clan could be killed!" Xiang Liang warned him. But inside, he knew that his nephew was no ordinary boy.

Xiang Yu was from a military family in the state of Chu. When he was less than 10 years old, Chu was conquered by the kingdom of Qin and China was unified.

But as the boy became bigger and stronger, his ambition grew as well. Soon, he would get his chance at greatness.

In 210 BC, the First Emperor died. In 209 BC, rebellions broke out and the Qin empire was weakened. Xiang Yu was 24.

That September, Xiang Liang held a discussion with the local governor, who wanted the Xiangs to fight for him, under his command. As Xiang Liang argued with him, Xiang Yu walked into the room and took matters into his own hands, killing not only the governor but dozens of his guards.

Holding the governor's head in one hand and his imperial seal in the other, Xiang Yu persuaded the surviving men to join him. These officers gathered 8,000 well-trained soldiers to join Xiang Liang's new army.

Xiang Yu, now second-in-command, marched north to cross the Yangtze River. More men eager to fight the Qin Dynasty joined and his ranks swelled to 60,000 or 70,000.

Meanwhile, the elderly counsellor Fan Zeng advised Xiang Liang to find Xiong Xin, the royal descendant of the old Chu king. They placed him on the throne as King Huai II, and the people celebrated the rebirth of their nation.

Xiang Liang clashed with Qin general Zhang Han, and was killed in battle. In 207 BC, Zhang's forces advanced north to attack the restored state of Zhao.

Instead of promoting Xiang Yu to replace his slain uncle, King Huai II ordered General Song Yi to take command of the army on its new mission: to save Zhao. The Chu forces went further north, reaching the Yellow River.

Burning with resentment, Xiang Yu murdered General Song and reported the matter to the king of Chu. Then he carried on with the mission.

In Chinese, to declare your intent to do something without turning back can be summed up in the phrase *po fu chen zhou*, or "smashing the cauldrons and sinking the boats." This comes from Xiang Yu's do-or-die moment at the Yellow River in the famous Battle of Julu.

Standing in the way of Xiang Yu and his men was a massive army of 300,000 well-trained Qin troops.

Xiang Yu, with limited men and even more limited

supplies, made one of the most famous plans in Chinese military history. After crossing the Yellow River, he ordered his men to sink their boats, smash their cauldrons and pots, and burn all their grain.

With no path of retreat, and the only possibility of survival ahead of them beyond the enemy lines, Chu troops fought like ferocious beasts. The Qin formations were overrun by this burst of raw power and collapsed after nine fierce battles. Xiang Yu's soldiers took 200,000 men prisoner.

Xiang Yu was a military man through and through. He spared no effort to give his comrades the best treatment and lead them with the best strategies. On the battlefield, he seemed unstoppable.

But to his enemies, even those who surrendered, he had no mercy. All 200,000 of the captured Qin troops were forced to dig their own graves. Then they were buried alive. The Qin generals Zhang Han and Sima Xin were allowed to live, and they joined Chu.

Because of his brutal character, Xiang Yu could have the strongest army in China and the best generals, but he would never be able to rule the land.

Xiang Yu was the greatest warrior in China at this time, but he was not content with being a mere general. He declared himself Hegemon King of Western Chu, and gave King Huai II the "more honorable" title of Emperor.

All the real power was in Xiang Yu's hands, but he was still not satisfied. He banished the "emperor" to his hometown and had him assassinated on the journey there.

Xiang Yu often failed to listen to or respect his allies and subordinates. When choosing where to locate his capital city, an advisor suggested the Qin imperial capital of Xianyang, because it was surrounded by mountains which formed a natural barrier against any foreign invasion. Ignoring him, Xiang Yu chose his hometown of Pengcheng, a city located at an important crossroads with few natural barriers essential for its defense.

"If I do not go home to show them how successful I am, that would be like wearing fine clothing under a moonless night," Xiang Yu explained.

The disappointed advisor said, "A monkey wearing clothes and hat is still a monkey. This is what the people of Chu are like, including Xiang Yu," he told a friend.

When Xiang Yu heard of the insult, he ordered the advisor to be boiled alive.

Thinking he had achieved victory after taking Xianyang, Xiang Yu proceeded to divide China into 18 different kingdoms. Xiang Yu was very loyal to his friends and appointed only people he liked personally to become kings, instead of basing it on their accomplishments in battle or other qualifications. Many generals who had allied with Xiang Yu to defeat the Qin came to hate him, as did the common people, who suffered wherever the Chu troops went.

To the west, Xiang Yu ordered warlord Liu Bang to rule the remote land of Han. At first, many of his men abandoned him, but he had his trusted advisors and the brilliant general Han Xin. Soon, Han conquered the old Qin lands, and was driving east and north.

If conquest of China depended on military strength alone,

Xiang Yu and Western Chu would have beaten the Han empire easily. In four years of warfare, Xiang Yu won nearly every battle he fought. On one occasion, Liu Bang led 500,000 soldiers to attack the city of Xingyang, but Xiang Yu needed just 30,000 men to drive them out.

But strategy is not just about raw fighting power. Xiang Yu was cruel to the common people, but Liu Bang treated them fairly. The Hegemon King rarely took advice from or promoted anyone he did not trust fully, but Liu Bang was willing to appoint an unknown genius like Han Xin into the general of his entire army. Xiang Yu acted like a warrior, but Liu Bang acted like an emperor.

Liu Bang and Han Xin sent their armies to conquer the kingdoms Xiang Yu had created. As Han grew, generals and kings on Xiang Yu's side saw fewer reasons to continue to follow him. Key men defected to Han, and Xiang Yu found his armies shrinking as soldiers ran off to join his adversaries..

Even Fan Zeng, the adviser who had helped Xiang Yu and his uncle get into power, became sick of this man who respectfully called him "second father" but did not heed his counsel. Finally, Xiang Yu fired him.

"The final outcome is obvious," Fan Zeng said ominously. "Take good care of yourself. Please allow me to retire in peace." The elderly man returned home and died from illness.

In 203 BC, the Han forces scored a major victory and pushed back the Chu armies to the east of the Hong Canal. They signed a peace treaty, but Western Chu was clearly disadvantaged since Han now controlled all of west, north, and central China.

Three days later, Liu Bang broke the treaty. Hundreds of thousands of Han troops swarmed the Chu homeland and attacked Xiang Yu's skilled but tired armies.

By 202 BC, Xiang Yu and his troops were surrounded in a canyon called Gaixia. The Han soldiers sang the folk songs of Chu, making the enemy feel homesick. In addition, Xiang Yu's men heard the songs and thought that many of their countrymen had joined the Han armies.

The Chinese phrase *si mian chu ge*—"Chu songs from four directions"—describes the despair that Xiang Yu and his men felt in their final days.

Xiang Yu was unable to sleep and began drinking alone in his camp. He sang heroic war songs in an attempt to brighten himself. But his lover, Lady Yu, knew the end was near. She sang a sad melody, then grabbed a sword and slit her throat. She did not want Xiang Yu to worry about her anymore.

With his lover lost and his homeland captured, Xiang Yu no longer had the will to keep fighting. He and 800 men managed to flee to the Wei River; by the time they got there, only 28 were left.

"It's not that I've fought poorly," Xiang Yu told his men. "But Heaven wills our defeat. Look, I will kill a Han general right now to show you."

He then charged out into the advancing Han soldiers, and indeed slew an enemy general. In the battle that followed, he and his 28 comrades killed hundreds of men while losing only two. The Han troops retreated in terror.

Xiang Yu then reached the Wu River, where a local official had already arranged a boat to secure an escape route back to his hometown.

Xiang Yu gazed far into the distance, towards his homeland. "I left home as the leader of 8,000 men," he wept. "Not one remains alive. I have no right to return and face their parents."

Then he told the official: "This horse has been with me for five years in battlefields all across China. He has never let me down. I can't bear to let him die with me. Please take him with you as my gift."

The Hegemon King and his men fought their final battle on the banks of the Wu. One by one they fell. Alone but unbeaten, Xiang Yu took down man after man. He spied among the Han troops an old friend, one among many who had left him to serve Liu Bang.

"Liu Bang put a reward on my head!" Xiang Yu bellowed to him. "Thousands of pieces of gold and a high post! Let me give you my head as my last gift!" This spoken, Xiang Yu killed himself.

So many Han soldiers struggled to claim the reward that Xiang Yu's body was cut to pieces. In the end, five men received the prize.

The Hegemon King Xiang Yu was a leader with many faults, a brilliant general but a poor politician. Even though he lost, Chinese people admired his refusal to give up. Hearing of Xiang Yu's death, Liu Bang wept and gave him a high posthumous rank to honor him. The well-known Beijing opera piece, "Farewell My Concubine," depicts his tragic romance with Lady Yu.

Emperor Wu of Han
The Emperor of War

ate at night in the year 138 BC, a gang of black-clad knights rode about in the mountains near the imperial capital of Chang'an. Chasing after wild beasts, they rode through fields belonging to local peasants, trampling the crops during the hunt. Local constables were informed and they summoned hundreds of soldiers to catch up with the mysterious horsemen.

The knights in black sent a delegate to handle the authorities. He told them that they were guards of a "Marquis of Pingyang", and would take financial responsibility for the damaged crops. The constables rejected this explanation, because there was no "Marquis of Pingyang" in Han China.

Just as the knights were about to be arrested and disarmed, the "Marquis" indeed appeared. He was less than 20 years old, but exuded an air of pride and nobility. When he showed the constables his seal, the officer in charge was shocked. The man was no marquis, but a man named Liu Che—Emperor Wu of the Han Dynasty. The name Wu means "war" and he was good at it.

Liu Che became emperor of the Han Dynasty at the age of 15, in the year 141 BC. Emperor Wu was very smart and in his childhood, he was said to have a photographic memory. Besides, he had a wide range of interests. He did not like to be trapped in the palace, so he often went out to observe his empire secretly. The black-clad knights were actually a special

scouting unit formed by the emperor personally. They would later become the basis for a new kind of imperial cavalry unit.

At the time, the Han empire, the fifth dynasty in Chinese history, was economically powerful and more prosperous than it had ever been. But the officials were corrupt and favored their own friends and family. Laws were not strict and there was a great gap between rich and poor.

After Liu Bang, also known as Emperor Gaozu of Han, created the dynasty in 206 B.C., he went to war with the fierce Xiongnu barbarians in northern Asia. He was trapped in the city of Pingcheng (modern-day Datong in Shanxi Province) by a powerful force of Xiongnu horsemen and only got out by trickery.

The Xiongnu Khan was fond of women, so Liu Bang's men painted a portrait of a beauty and sent it to him, explaining that Liu Bang was ready to surrender and that the pictured woman would soon be his. But when the Khan's wife found out, she went wild with jealousy. The Khan had to pull out his troops to appease her. Liu Bang then escaped.

From here on, the Han Dynasty, with its inferior military strength, had to buy peace from the Xiongnu by giving them princesses and beautiful women as tribute every so often. This was another humiliation that China had suffered for many years by the time Emperor Wu took the throne.

Emperor Wu wanted to reform the country, but most of the high officials were against him. Real power was held by the Grand Empress, who was Liu Che's grandmother. She even had control over the army because she held the so-called "tiger tally," which was needed to approve all military orders and troop mobilizations.

For political reasons, Liu Che was forced to marry his cousin, Empress Chen, who was eight years older than him, spoiled, and had a greedy and corrupt mother. Chen could not have children, but she was jealous and did not allow Liu to have imperial concubines. Because of this, many officials wondered if the emperor was capable of fathering sons to continue the dynasty.

Liu Che knew that he was alone in facing powerful forces. He pretended to be uninterested in politics, and spent his days hunting and sightseeing. He could not trust anyone in the imperial court, so he created a secret circle of ministers. Members of this "inner" court, as it is called in the historical documents, came from ordinary Chinese society and were highly loyal to the emperor. They held various positions in the imperial government and reported to Emperor Wu in secret.

An opportunity came when rebellions broke out in eastern China. Even though he did not have the tiger tally, Liu Che had some supporters in the army who carried out his orders.

These soldiers came back victorious, and Liu was seen as a fine leader.

In the meantime, Liu became bold enough to oppose Empress Chen. He fell in love with Wei Zifu (pronounced "way zz-fu"), a lowly but delightful palace maid, and she became pregnant. This proved to skeptical officials that Emperor Wu could, in fact, produce an heir. Wei Zifu became Empress.

In 135 BC, Liu's grandmother, the Grand Empress, died. Emperor Wu was in command.

During the reigns of the emperors between Liu Bang and Liu Che, the Han Dynasty government had built up so much wealth in its treasuries that the strings used to tie coins together (ancient Chinese coins had square holes in the center) were rotting away.

With all this money, Emperor Wu vowed to make China's armed forces powerful enough to take on the Xiongnu and reasserted its imperial authority.

The entire Xiongnu population was just one million, but they had 300,000 highly skilled horsemen. Xiongnu men spent their entire lives on the plains, learning horseback riding and archery from as young as they learned to speak.

By Emperor Wu's time, the Xiongnu no longer respected Chinese borders. Often they would find a point along the Great Wall, bash a hole in it, and send a raiding force deep into Han territory to loot wealth and take slaves. On one occasion, they were as close as 100 kilometers away from Chang'an.

Used to spending their time growing crops in the fields

or studying, Chinese soldiers did not stack up against the nomadic warriors. Chinese horses had little space to graze. Next to the wild steeds of the Mongolian plain, they looked more like ponies.

Emperor Wu needed to change this if he was going to defeat the barbarian nomads.

Liu Che ordered a Chinese force of 300,000 men to lie in wait in the mountains, then ambush the Xiongnu cavalry when they attacked a nearby city. Unfortunately, the Xiongnu took some Han officers prisoner, who divulged the plan before the operation could be carried out. The Han-Xiongnu wars that would last about 200 years had begun.

While the Xiongnu had the superior cavalry, China also had its strengths. First, the Han Dynasty's population was over 50 million. There was no shortage of manpower.

Second, the empire's massive wealth meant that it could support large armies in the field with all the food, weapons, and supplies they would ever need. The Xiongnu, meanwhile, had to keep attacking and looting Chinese cities in order to replenish their stocks.

Emperor Wu ordered his brand-new expeditionary cavalry five times to attack the Xiongnu on their own territory. Each time the Xiongnu would fight for a while, and retreat further north.

The Chinese army was determined to find out how far the Xiongnu could go. In 119 BC, the emperor dispatched 21-year-old cavalry general Huo Qubing to pursue the nomads. Leading 20,000 horsemen, Huo crossed the vast Gobi Desert, and finally encountered the Xiongnu in their heartland. In several battles, the Chinese army killed and wounded 70,000 enemies, and 83 Xiongnu leaders were captured. Huo Qubing's troops also confiscated 400,000 sheep from the nomads.

Huo's troops kept marching. They passed Mongolia and did not turn back until they reached the shores of Lake Baikal in what is now Siberia.

The operation was a resounding success, so Emperor Wu sent Huo Qubing out again and again, for a total of seven expeditionary missions. The only thing that stopped Huo from going out an eighth time was disease. In 117 BC, Huo Qubing died at the age of just 23. Emperor Wu was devastated and had a grand tomb constructed for the young general. A large stone statue was built in his honor and given the impressive name of "Horse Stomping the Xiongnu."

At the other end was the old general Li Guang. An expert archer, Li could hit a leaf at a distance of a hundred steps. Born into a military family, he had prepared to fight the Xiongnu for many years. But in actual combat, Li Guang did not shine. He and his troops were defeated multiple times and Li Guang was even captured once.

In one final battle, Li Guang, aged 71, pleaded with the emperor to give him one more chance. He led an army out to meet the enemy, but his troops got lost on the way. By the time he arrived on the field, the battle was over. Unable to bear the shame, Li Guang committed suicide.

His grandson Li Ling saw greater success. The emperor had held him in high regard since he was a child and allowed him to command of an army despite his grandfather's failures.

In 99 BC, Li Ling led a force of 5,000 infantry on an expedition to attack the Xiongnu. In the confusion of the operation, the reinforcements that Li was supposed to receive never arrived. When they spotted a 30,000-strong force of Xiongnu cavalry on the horizon, they thought the end had come.

But Li's troops were armed with an advanced technology: the repeating crossbow. It could shoot faster, farther, and more accurately than normal bows. As the Xiongnu got near, the Chinese foot soldiers simply aimed and shot. In about a week, eight thousand Xiongnu horsemen were wiped out as they charged at Li Ling's army on the grassland.

The Great Khan of the Xiongnu was overcome with anger when he heard that a mere infantry force had destroyed his cavalry. He ordered nearly 100,000 horsemen to attack Li Ling's force, which was running low on arrows and men. By the time they ran out completely, just 1,000 Han soldiers were left.

With no way out of the encircling Xiongnu forces, Li Ling surrendered. The Xiongnu Khan was impressed by this Chinese general and made him a minor king. One imperial report claimed that Li even helped train the Xiongnu soldiers, which led to further Chinese defeats in the east.

This was not true, but Emperor Wu was enraged. To punish Li for his betrayal, his entire clan was executed. Even his 80-year-old grandmother was not spared.

Li Ling surrendered because based on the standing orders, no Han soldier was allowed to retreat from battle. Even though he had never received the reinforcements he deserved, and had fought valiantly, the rule still applied to Li. In the end, he married a Xiongnu woman and considered himself a nomad.

After Emperor Wu died, many of Li's friends and comrades received high posts in the Han military and government, but

Li never returned to China. The tribe he joined settled in what is now Kyrgyzstan and did not get into further conflicts with Han.

In addition to fighting the Xiongnu, China under Emperor Wu expanded its territory west and south. After the Qin Dynasty fell, parts of southern China and northern Vietnam had broken off and became independent. This empire is called Nan Yue in Chinese and Nam Viet in Vietnamese. Its first king was Qin Dynasty general Zhao Tuo, but his descendants mixed Chinese and local culture during the 100 years that their nation existed.

The later kings of Nan Yue rejected their Chinese heritage. In 112 BC, Emperor Wu sent out a Han army of 100,000 men to conquer Nan Yue.

In the west, Emperor Wu sent explorers to chart the vast regions of Central Asia and the dozens of small states there. Many of these kingdoms pledged allegiance to the Han and the Silk Road to the Middle East and Europe was established.

43 years of war had undoubtedly taken their tolls on both China and the Xiongnu. The nomads were not completely defeated, but they were no longer a serious threat to Han. The Xiongnu government was also in disorder from the repeated assaults carried out on their land. The southern part surrendered to Han and the northern Xiongnu continued their troublesome raids on a smaller scale.

Emperor Wu put a temporary halt to his military expansion. He issued a public statement apologizing to the people for bringing them hardship.

Warfare and conquest was a key feature in Emperor Wu's rule, but it was not the only aspect. China continued to prosper under his reign, and he introduced extremely important cultural and political reforms.

Before Emperor Wu, Chinese government followed a lighter version of Qin's Legalist policies mixed with the relaxed, freedom-loving traditions of the Taoist religion. During Wu's rule, he spent much money to promote music, art, and literature. He also hired the brilliant scholar Dong Zhongshu.

Dong Zhongshu followed the teachings of Confucius, who believed that people would live in harmony if there was universal respect for elders, rituals, and moral standards. Dong took this a step further and believed that the government should do more to encourage proper behavior and thinking, just as though the entire empire were one family. Emperor Wu also subscribed to these ideas and had them become the official philosophy of the Han Dynasty.

Qin Shi Huang unified China's politics, language, and measurements, but Emperor Wu turned China into a military, geographic, and cultural superpower, on par with the Roman Empire in terms of military strength but surpassing it in its influence.

Confucianism was the Han government's ideology and united the common people with their rulers. Taoism continued to flourish and Buddhism was later introduced to China through India via the Silk Road.

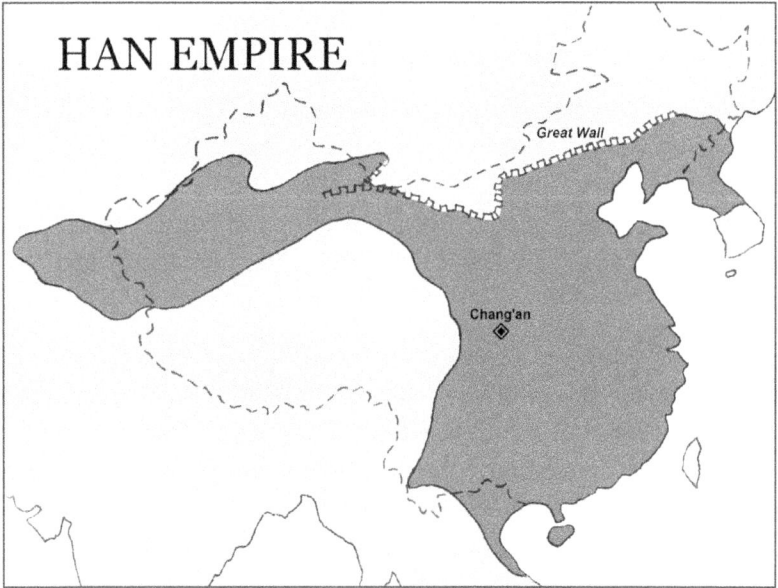

The Han Dynasty was a true superpower. Emperor Wu defeated the Xiongnu nomads and connected China with the West via the Silk Road.

23

Su Wu and Zhang Qian
Explorers of the Great Han

In the year 138 BC, about 100 horsemen rode forth from the gates of Chang'an, capital of Han China.

The leader of this cavalry team was a man named Zhang Qian, someone we know as the first Chinese diplomat. He was sent on this secret mission by the 18-year-old Liu Che, better known as Emperor Wu.

The unified China was strong and prosperous, with vast territory and a vibrant economy. Emperor Wu's greatest wish, however, was to see an end to the continual attacks by the Xiongnu empire along China's northern borders. The Xiongnu people and their warriors were a nomadic race and constantly moved between the north and the west. It was impossible to gather much intelligence about them, especially to the western regions where few Chinese had ventured.

As one of the emperor's military aides, Zhang Qian loved travel and adventure. Spending all his time in the imperial palace was incredibly depressing, so it delighted him to learn of Emperor Wu's plan to send men to the western regions. The emperor too was glad to find a soldier willing to venture through uncharted desert routes filled with hostile and fierce tribes, so he gave Zhang Qian a stash of treasure and 100 men to lead on his journey.

Far to the west was the Yuezhi people. This country used to be closer to China, but the Xiongnu attacked it and killed its king, forcing the entire people to move into what is now Kazakhstan.

The Yuezhi could be of aid to China's hundred-year-war with the Xiongnu, Emperor Wu thought. Zhang Qian's mission was to contact the Yuezhi and get them on board.

Zhang and his men's secondary objective was to locate a mystical breed of horse, stronger and faster than those available in China. Dubbed the Celestial Steed, it was expected that these prized beasts would be able to help the Chinese match the renowned cavalry of the Xiongnu.

Zhang Qian set off to the west, but he would not return home until 13 years later.

But while passing through the Tian Shan mountains, the Chinese mission was quickly ambushed and attacked by the Xiongnu horsemen. Zhang Qian was brought before the Great Khan of the Xiongnu and imprisoned.

Instead of killing him, the Khan treated him as a guest of honor. He hoped Zhang could stay and serve the Xiongnu. To make him feel at home, they even gave him a Xiongnu beauty to be his wife.

Zhang Qian lived among the Xiongnu for 10 years and had children. But he was still loyal to Emperor Wu and Han China.

One moonless and windy night, Zhang snuck out of the camp with a translator, leaving behind his wife and their children. Finally, he reached the kingdom of Yuezhi.

The Yuezhi received Zhang Qian with respect and graciousness, but made it clear that they were not interested in forming any kind of military pact with the Hans.

Zhang Qian's mission was over, and he began the long journey back to Chang'an. He took a different route, but was captured yet again. This time, he remained captive for a year before escaping and returning to Chang'an in 125 BC.

Even though Zhang failed to achieve the two objectives since he never discovered the "celestial steeds", his journey west opened the eyes of the Han imperial court to the possibility of trade and closer relations with the Central Asian people. This marked the beginning of the famous Silk Road. Goods from China reached all the way to the Roman Empire.

Zhang Qian himself was eager to go on a second trip to the west. This time, he brought more men and supplies, and the route was safer since part of it was now occupied by Han armies. Zhang contacted more kingdoms, including Wusun. The following generations opened up more trade and contact across the deserts and mountains, extending China's influence westwards and bringing back exotic goods from Central Asia.

The Silk Road was the main avenue of trade and contact between East and West for over 1,000 years, until the Europeans began to explore the seas.

About twenty years after Zhang Qian made his second trip, Emperor Wu heard that the Xiongnu had chosen a new Khan and decided to try making peace with him. The emperor again sent out a diplomatic mission of about 100 men.

Their leader this time was Su Wu, a commander in the imperial guard. He brought gifts for the Xiongnu, as well as an imperial staff to show his position.

But the new Khan was skeptical and rude. Su Wu's second-in-command Zhang Sheng was angry and began a plot with some of the Khan's officials. They hatched a plan to kill a Xiongnu minister and replace the Khan himself.

The plot failed. The Khan had Zhang put to death, but spared Su Wu because he was impressed with his strong character. He wanted Su to give up Han China and work for the Xiongnu instead. The proud imperial officer refused immediately.

As a result, the Xiongnu Khan exiled him to the "northern sea" where Lake Baikal, part of the vast territory of Siberian Russia, is today. Over 1,000 years before Russia even existed, Su Wu was the first prisoner known to be exiled to this freezing wasteland.

Su Wu began to starve. To survive, Su Wu fed on wild roots and hunted rodents. But he still clutched his imperial staff and refused the Xiongnu's many offers.

The news that came from home just added to Su's torment. Emperor Wu was dead after 60 years on the throne. Su Wu's brothers had been accused of crimes and committed suicide. His mother had died and his wife was now married to another man.

In 81 BC, 19 years after Su Wu left China, the Han Dynasty finally succeeded in making peace with the Xiongnu. Su Wu returned home with his hair all gray and his imperial staff reduced to a simple wooden rod. All the decorations had worn off, but he received a personal reception from Emperor Zhao, youngest son of the late Emperor Wu.

24

Wang Zhaojun
The beauty who brought peace

During the reign of Emperor Yuan in the Han Dynasty, there was a girl called Wang Zhaojun. It was said that wherever she went, birds in flight would forget to flap their wings and fall to earth upon seeing her. She came from a village in what is now central China's Hubei Province, and was a local celebrity. In the year 36 BC, she was selected to enter the imperial palace.

In addition to their main empress and several imperial consorts, ancient Chinese emperors had many, sometimes thousands of women in the palace. In order to get an idea of the girls living in his great residence, the emperor had to rely on official court painters to provide him with their portraits,

Palace ladies often came from rich families who wanted to get closer to the emperor. To make the best impression, many parents bribed the court artists to depict their daughters as fairer and more beautiful. The portraits received by the emperor were generally not how the woman actually looked, but how much her family paid the artist.

Wang Zhaojun was confident in her looks and did not bribe the artist. As a reprisal, the latter painted a mole on her portrait which made her look ugly. On top of that, the mole was placed in a position that was believed to bring bad luck to whoever married her.

For the next three years, Zhaojun lived in the palace without meeting a single man.

In 33 BC, exactly 100 years after Emperor Wu launched total war on the Xiongnu, a large group of horsemen met with the forward troops of the Han army. In command of the riders was Huhanye Chanyu, a Xiongnu chief. He was here in China not to wage war, but to make peace with the emperor.

A century of fighting had worn down the Xiongnu and the nomads themselves was no longer one state. Instead, they had split up in five tribes, and each one was run by a Chanyu, which meant "chief" or "leader" in the ancient Mongol language that the Xiongnu spoke.

Huhanye Chanyu, who led the southernmost of the Xiongnu tribes, decided to acknowledge the Han Dynasty and become a Chinese ally. The united forces of the Han and southern Xiongnu dealt the Zhizhi Chanyu of the northern Xiongnu a humiliating defeat, and he fled west to Central Asia.

In 40 BC, the Huhanye Chanyu asked permission to visit the Chinese imperial capital in Chang'an, so that he could give thanks to the emperor in person—the first time in history that a foreign leader made a formal trip to China. He was received by the Han imperial court. The emperor even came out of the palace to personally greet him.

During the visit, the emperor granted the chanyu and his country many gifts, including grain, silk, fine cloth, and money to help the nomads through harsh times.

Very pleased, the chanyu made another visit several years later. This time he asked to marry into the Han imperial family, so that he could defend China's northern frontier as a proper member of the imperial court.

Emperor Yuan granted this request, but there was a problem: no Chinese princess would want to leave her home to live among the unfamiliar terrain and culture of the Mongolian plains.

The emperor had to find someone from among his palace maids to go on the journey and marry the Huhanye chanyu. To encourage them, the emperor ordered that anyone willing to go would be considered a princess of the imperial family.

Wang Zhaojun volunteered for the assignment. When Emperor Yuan had a look at her official portrait, he saw a plain-looking woman with an unlucky mole on her face. He would not miss her.

In 33 BC, Wang Zhaojun was formally introduced to the chanyu at the imperial palace. Huhanye had no idea that the emperor would allow him to marry such a beautiful woman. He swore an oath on the spot to never betray the Han empire.

Emperor Yuan was also shocked, but his reaction was one of anger and regret. He wondered how he had failed to notice that this girl of incomparable beauty had been living among his palace maidens.

According to the official history, Emperor Yuan tracked down the court artist who had painted Zhaojun's portrait, and had him executed.

But Wang Zhaojun was well and gone forever. As she crossed the Great Wall, she burned incense and kowtowed to her homeland and family, whom she would never see again.

Wang Zhaojun spent 50 years living with the Xiongnu, and had a son with the chanyu. Unfortunately, the chanyu died just three years after marrying her. The new chanyu was

Huhanye's son by a different wife, and according to Xiongnu custom, men could marry their stepmothers if they became widows.

Zhaojun was queen of the Xiongnu for long after her original husband died. She had two daughters with the new chanyu. For the 50 years that she lived among the Xiongnu, both the Hans and the nomads enjoyed peace.

When Wang Zhaojun died, the Xiongnu mourned and buried her near the border with China. Her grave faces south, towards the homeland she left behind.

Besides Zhaojun, Chinese dynasties sent other beautiful women to please the leaders of foreign tribes. Seventy years earlier, in 105 BC, when the Han empire was bitterly at war with the Xiongnu, Emperor Wu (Emperor Yuan's grandfather) desperately needed allies. So he sent the princess Liu Xijun to the kingdom of Wusun, a desert country thousands of miles to the west. Unlike Zhaojun, she was not able to adapt to the strange culture and language of her new family. Liu Xijun was constantly homesick, as revealed in her sorrowful poem:

> *My family's married me off to the other side of heaven,*
> *I'm in a strange land, cared for by the Wusun king.*
> *A round tent is my room, and my walls are made of felt,*
> *I eat the meat of beasts and drink the milk of beasts.*
> *It breaks my heart to live here and constantly think of home,*
> *I wish to become a yellow heron and make my way back.*

Sadly, Liu Xijun died only after four or five years in Wusun, when she was only in her twenties. Emperor Wu sent another lady, Liu Jieyou, who married the Wusun king and had five children. The Wusun allied with the Han Dynasty and helped it defeat the northern Xiongnu tribes.

Liu Jieyou lived in Wusun for 50 years and had two husbands there. At age 70, she asked to retire and made the tough trip back to China. She passed away peacefully in Chang'an.

But Liu Jieyou would not have been so successful were it

not for her friend and attendant Feng Liao, another beauty who accompanied her on the trip. Feng was very intelligent and acted as Jieyou's representative. She handled all the complex diplomatic issues between the Wusun kingdom and China, which made the alliance possible. Because of her charm, the northern Xiongnu tribes never broke into China's western frontier.

25
Chen Tang
The Han Dynasty's Wild West

For Chinese generals fighting in the desert thousands of kilometers away from the imperial capital, adapting to tough situations often required taking the law into their own hands.

Around the year 40 BC, centuries of war between the Chinese Han Dynasty and northern barbarians was finally coming to a close.

A lowly frontier commander, Chen Tang, committed the crime of overthrowing his superior officer—an offense punishable by death—but doing this enabled him to score final victory over the Xiongnu nomads.

Chen was born and grew up in one of the poorest families in Jiaozuo, city in the mountains of what is now Henan Province. Penniless and impoverished, Chen and his family lived on the charity of generous neighbors and friends, borrowing bits and scraps from whoever they could.

Naturally, no one in Jiaozuo thought highly of the destitute young Chen. Yet one thing made the boy stand out—he loved reading, and when given brush and paper, he was articulate and brimming with ideas.

Unfortunately for Chen, continuing his studies was impossible when his next meal was constantly in question. Drifting about, he eventually set his foot in Chang'an, the capital of Han China.

Chang'an was full of talents from near and far. Chen soon befriended people of various circles, including the nobleman Marquis Zhang Bo. As it happened, the imperial ministers were aging and the emperor was in need of young and gifted men to replenish the ranks.

Seizing the opportunity, Zhang recommended Chen for office.

But just as he was about to land the job, a tragedy got in the way: Chen's father died. By law, subjects of the Han Dynasty had to return home and tend the graves of their parents for three years to express respect and mourn for the dead.

The ambitious Chen Tang would not have any of that, especially not when fame and fortune were so close at hand. He disobeyed the law and stayed in Chang'an.

It was no small mistake. Filial piety was not only a duty expected of citizens, it was a reflection of one's moral character. Chen's unfilial act was discovered and reported. Chen not only lost his government position but earned a prison sentence as well. His friend, Marquis Zhang, was also punished for recommending such a man.

While Chen sat in prison contemplating his plight, the Han empire faced new disturbances in its faraway western territories.

A Han expeditionary force had attacked and weakened the Xiongnu tribes, but the new chieftain who took power among the nomads was a man who hated the Han empire to the bone. Called Zhizhi, he found and took every opportunity he could to challenge the imperial authority.

Zhizhi imprisoned one Chinese envoy and murdered a

second, which was tantamount to declaring war. Zhizhi was not strong enough to face the imperial army, so he fled west to the remote Kangju Kingdom (between present day Xinjiang Province and Kazakhstan) and became a local tyrant.

Further defying Han China, Zhizhi led his men to kill and rob the people of kingdoms and tribes that pledged allegiance to the Han emperor.

The Chinese sent more messengers to try and resolve the situation. Zhizhi only laughed at them: "Life in this remote area doesn't suit me. Maybe I should join the Han and have my son enter the imperial palace."

For the Xiongnu chieftain, this was a sarcastic way of saying that he would like to replace the Chinese emperor. When the messenger returned to Chang'an, the imperial court was enraged.

Around this time, Chen Tang had finished serving his sentence in prison and was itching to restart his career. Politics was not an option, so he volunteered to defend the imperial frontier. Chen made a forty-day march under scorching heat to get to his outpost in the desert.

In 36 BC, Chen became second-in-command of several thousand men under the leadership of officer Gan Yanshou.

Chen was bold and intelligent. Whether it was a town, a mountain or a river he passed by, not a single detail escaped his eyes. He did not dream of achieving big goals all the time. But how would that be possible with just a few thousand border guards under his command?

Two years later, Chen got his chance. General Gan fell ill and turned command over to his deputy. Chen wasted no time. He forged an imperial edict and summoned all soldiers guarding the border to his own outpost. Tens of thousands of men, belonging to both Han imperial armies and the bands of the allied kingdoms, started their march into battle. Soon Chen Tang had 40,000 troops.

On his sickbed, a startled General Gan tried to stop Chen's outrageous action. But with his voice stern and sword in hand, Chen said, "The assembled troops are already on their way. Do you want to hold us back? What kind of commander backs off from a coming battle?"

Seeing that the die was cast, Gan yielded. He sent a letter to Chang'an to apologize for faking the imperial order, and the

allied forces marched north.

Now commander of the troops, Chen set his sights on the Kangju kingdom—Zhizhi's lair. Along the 1,500-kilometer (900 miles) trek, the army passed through the friendly kingdom of Wusun. Nobles from the royal family helped Chen learn the terrain and gather information about the enemy.

Finally, Chen's forces reached Tucheng, a city under Zhizhi's occupation. But Chen knew that to take on the walled fortress, he would have to catch the enemy off guard.

Meanwhile, Zhizhi heard the arrival of Chen's 40,000 men and considered retreat. But instead of a proud Chinese army, what the Xiongnu warriors saw were tired and disorganized men staggering towards the city gates. Zhizhi abandoned his plans. Now he just laughed alongside his minions from the high walls of the city.

But from Chen's perspective, everything was going according to plan. While the Xiongnu jeered, the Han troops slowly surrounded the city. It was time to strike.

Before Zhizhi knew it, arrows flew forth like rainfall, slaying the inattentive Xiongnu soldiers one after another. Zhizhi himself received a serious wound when an arrow caught him in the face. In the next battle, he lost his head.

Chen's unauthorized war ended the threat from the Xiongnu that had pestered China for the last 300 years. In high spirits, Chen declared: "No matter how far away, whoever dares to offend the Han empire must die."

On their return, the triumphant troops were halted by an officer from Chang'an. The emperor heard that Chen pocketed seized treasures and had sent him to investigate, the officer announced.

Chen was rather put off. "We marched thousands of miles to fight Zhizhi and defend our country; yet rather than appreciation, we are greeted with interrogation and arrests. Are you getting revenge on behalf of our enemies?"

Somewhat abashed, the emperor called back the officer, asking that local county magistrate set out welcoming banquets along their journey.

Although the emperor had pardoned Chen Tang and General Gan, their crime of forging imperial orders was not easily forgotten. A good number of councilors insisted on executing them to warn those who broke the law. It was one sympathetic official who saved them. The victory was "a glory that would shine for thousands of years, securing peace on the frontier for all ages," he said. They accomplished what all had attempted and failed to achieve, he added. Because of his persistence, Emperor Yuan rewarded Gan and Chen the title of marquis. They were made generals and rewarded by gold.

The victory over Chief Zhizhi was a milestone in Chinese history. The northern Xiongnu tribes fled further north and west. Three hundred years later, Attila the Hun emerged in Europe as the chief of a nomadic group that may have come from the Xiongnu. He united many other tribes and went on a path of conquest, causing the fall of the powerful Roman Empire.

26

Wang Mang
A tongue that tricked the empire with sweet lies

The only emperor in Chinese history who founded a dynasty without waging war was Wang Mang, the first and only ruler of the Xin Dynasty. He did it in the middle of the Han Dynasty, splitting the empire's history between the Western (earlier) and Eastern (later) periods.

Wang Mang's family was a powerful clan with great fame and influence. His aunt was the empress.

He could have enjoyed many luxuries, but Wang Mang led a simple life of hard work and study. From his teachers, he learned the classics of Confucius. He was a responsible man who took care of his mother and sister-in-law, as well as her children. A strict and natural leader, he became well-known for being respectful to his family and especially his elders, and was a gentleman when dealing with outsiders.

Wang Mang soon became an officer of the imperial guard. His rise continued until he became one of the emperor's trusted advisers. Though his position was very powerful, Wang Mang remained polite and close to his friends and subordinates, and he kept his clean and frugal habits. Sometimes, he would split his salary and distribute it among the common people. On one occasion, he even sold his horse and carriage and gave the money to the poor.

Both the common people and officials praised Wang for his character. His prestige exceeded even that of the elders in his powerful family.

After a few years, one of Wang Mang's uncles, a Minister of War, decided to retire. He successfully persuaded the emperor to replace him with Wang Mang, who became the new minister at age 38. When the emperor bestowed gifts upon him, he would never take them home, but instead use them for the public good. On one occasion, his mother fell ill, and the wives of many court officials came to pay her a visit. These noble ladies were dripping with gold and silver, but Wang Mang's wife was wearing clothes of a coarse fabric, and her dress was barely long enough to cover her knees. Many guests wondered if she was a maid.

Wang Mang was not afraid to preach his ideas. He asked his aunt, who was the emperor's mother, to take the lead and live a simpler, more frugal life. Wang himself donated millions in cash and over hundreds of acres of land to the poor. Others did the same. Whenever the empire suffered drought or floods, Wang Mang would stop eating meat or drinking wine. One year, the country was hit by a drought and to make matters worse, a plague of locusts destroyed the crop. Many common people were forced to leave their homes and beg for food. Wang and 230 other officials and wealthy businessmen donated their land and estates to the starving poor. He even converted an imperial forest preserve into a refugee town, and set up 1,000 dwellings for refugees in the middle of the imperial capital.

People began to compare Wang to the legendary sage emperors Yao and Shun, who worked tirelessly and selflessly for the good of the country.

But as time passed, Wang Mang began to show his dark side.

When the emperor died, Wang Mang resigned from his post and lived a life of seclusion to avoid any political struggles.

One day, Wang found out that his second son had murdered a slave. In anger, Wang forced his son to commit suicide to pay for his crime. This act of justice, even against his own family, earned Wang a new level of respect among the government, and many officials requested that the emperor restore his official rank.

A few years later, Wang got his post back, but he was concerned that the new emperor's mother and her family

might interfere with his power. To prevent this, Wang had the emperor's mother and her kin exiled to faraway places and forbade them from visiting Chang'an, the imperial capital.

Wang's older son was worried that the emperor would take revenge, so he did his best to try to get his father to back down. Wang did not listen, so his son planned a strange act. He told his brother-in-law to spill blood-red wine all over the gate of Wang Mang's mansion to get his attention and persuade him to mend his ways.

Wang Mang discovered the "warning" his son planned. In a fit of rage, he threw his son behind bars and had him poisoned to death. Soon afterward, he also had the emperor's mother and her entire family killed. Then he slaughtered several hundreds of officials and other nobility who opposed his ideas, including a princess, whom he forced to commit suicide. These brutal acts shocked the whole empire.

To justify all this violence, Wang Mang had his subordinates spread the idea that the killings were a great campaign to punish the criminal deeds of his family and put the law above his personal interests. Writings that glorified Wang's actions were distributed to all parts of the empire and recorded in official historical records. Everyone from officials to commoners had to memorize them.

Wang Mang was already the most powerful official in the Han empire, but he did not stop there. Since the new emperor was young, Wang decided to make him marry his daughter. In the meantime, Wang used his control over the throne to practise his ideology, which included the construction of huge marketplaces and ten thousand homes in the imperial capital. He invited thousands of talents and artists to reside there. Wang promoted a version of the code of ethics that Confucius had taught, winning the allegiance of intellectuals and scholars.

Everyone seemed to worship Wang Mang. Half a million officials and common people petitioned the emperor to reward him. Among his supporters were nine hundred high-ranking ministers who bestowed upon him the finest horses and carriages, expensive robes and ornaments, top-class musical instruments, great doors covered in crimson lacquer, special red and black bows and arrows, a gold plaque giving him an imperial license to kill, and fine wines normally reserved for the exclusive use of the emperor.

Following this, Wang Mang sent eight "popular envoys" on missions across the country. They returned to the imperial court with stories that all under heaven was peaceful and prosperous, and said that this was the successful outcome of Wang's teachings. Wang Mang then expended massive sums of money to convince the Xiongnu and other barbarian tribes to pledge their loyalty to Han.

In the eyes of the people, all this made Wang Mang a great sage whose rule brought peace to the country. Then the young emperor suddenly died (it has been rumored that Wang killed him by poisoning his wine), and Wang immediately made the two-year-old Liu Ying crown prince. Because Wang had a good relationship with the dead emperor's mother, she let him rule in place of the baby monarch.

The Liu family, the imperial family of the Han Dynasty, opposed this. Two members of the family attempted rebellion, which scared Wang terribly. He was unable to eat well and spent day and night praying in temple with the emperor at his side. He also wrote an article claiming that his position as proxy emperor was merely a temporary role, to be given up once Liu Ying came of age to rule by himself.

But as Wang made these promises, he deployed armies to crush the nobles' rebellion.

As he was getting rid of these hindrances, he began to harbor secret plans to become the emperor. Besides this, many people with their own motives were telling him to take the throne.

Finally, the once-modest Wang Mang went to the

emperor's mother and forced her to hand over the imperial seal of the Han court.

In the year AD 8, Wang Mang officially became emperor and changed the name of the dynasty to "*Xin*," which means "new."

As emperor, many of Wang Mang's policies resembled the modern ideas of socialism. The Xin Dynasty lasted only 16 years.

Wang Mang read many ancient books from a young age, and believed that the empire would be at peace only when the code of ethics from the Western Zhou Dynasty were restored. This led him to do many things that, when looked at from a normal point of view, seem completely senseless.

First, he abolished the old coins used in the Han Dynasty. The chaos this act caused, brought down the Chinese financial system.

The second thing he tried was to make all land property of the imperial family, following what was done in the Western Zhou times, a thousand years before. Wang's intention was to take land from powerful landlords and give it to those in need. The landlords resisted and in many cases refused to hand over their land. The new emperor had no choice but to abandon this plan.

The third thing Wang Mang did was to outlaw the slave trade. Though this seems like a good idea in theory, the former slaves kept their old social identity, and did not gain the support of the common people. In fact, it caused great anger among those in the middle class. Three years later, Wang Mang was forced to re-legalize slavery.

Wang Mang also introduced various programs to change the society and economy. For example, people could take out loans from the government at very modest interest rates. Some important industries, like salt, metalworking, brewing, and coin minting were completely taken over by the government. All land not owned privately was automatically government property, and anyone who wanted to develop it would have to pay expensive taxes.

Many of these policies did not match up with reality. The land area that the Han Dynasty controlled was too vast and the population too large to be governed the way Wang hoped. He had to summon a massive number of middle and low ranking officials to carry out his detailed plans, something that there was nowhere near enough money for, even in the imperial coffers. The only way was to rely on rich merchants and the upper class to help out. Their actions were unsupervised, so when it came to carrying out the emperor's policies, it was actually a unique opportunity to fleece the common people.

Instead of helping the masses as he hoped, Wang's policies harmed them and damaged the entire economy of the empire.

Wang Mang was obsessed with the ancient past. He tried to change the empire to reflect the ways of the ancients in every way possible. He started by reviving the ancient forms of Chinese writing and titles. The names of cities, regions, official ranks, and buildings were reverted back to names that nobody had used for hundreds of years. Some places had their names altered multiple times in the same year; sometimes, for whatever reason the name was changed, then restored to its original name. In any case, the changes confused both officials and commoners. In official and formal documents, it became a habit to write the original name of places behind the official name.

Wang's obsession with "proper" wording also caused huge problems in relations with foreign tribes. At the time, China had provinces named for seas of the north, east, and south. To fix the lack of a West Sea Province, Wang forced the Qiang people of the northwest to "offer" him the lands around Lake Qinghai and create an imperial province out of it, called Xihai, which means "West Sea."

The "Chinese" province was full of foreigners, so to solve this problem, Wang Mang created over 50 new criminal laws. As a result, many Chinese became guilty of crimes, which allowed Wang to exile them to the newly-created West Sea Province.

Wang acted arrogantly to non-Chinese leaders who had pledged their allegiance to the Han Dynasty. This included the Xiongnu to the north, the Koreans in the east, and the various rulers of western and southern tribes. Before, the imperial court recognized these leaders as kings, but Wang informed them that they were from now on only worthy of being called dukes.

Unsurprisingly, many of these leaders refused to acknowledge Wang's Xin Dynasty.

In the 13th year of Wang's rule, all kinds of revolts popped up with people forming their own armies to fight imperial rule. Not only this, but China was also caught up in a cascade of natural disasters. Besides plagues, locusts, and droughts, the Yellow River flooded, causing massive famine. Peasants across the empire rose in revolt. Wang Mang was no general and had no experience in commanding armies. Instead, he and his followers gathered to pray to heaven and sob for the earth while reading off lists of the emperor's achievements, hoping that the gods would be moved and use lightning to exterminate the rebels. Obviously, this was useless, and the rebellions only grew in strength.

In October of the year 23, a group of rebels who vowed to bring back the Han Dynasty launched a massive attack on the imperial capital of Chang'an. Wang Mang had no choice but to throw open the prison gates and release the criminals, who were then drafted into the army after being made to drink pig-blood wine and swear an oath of loyalty to the Xin Dynasty.

This defense failed. The army of criminals disintegrated on first contact with the enemy.

As rebels closed in, Wang Mang and a thousand of his closest followers were betrayed and slaughtered by a merchant they had trusted. Wang's head was cut off and hung over the streets. Soldiers chopped off parts of his body. Some even cut out his tongue, saying that this was the tongue that had tricked everybody in the empire with sweet lies.

Wang Mang brought the Han Dynasty to the brink of disaster. But after his death, it came back to life and continued for the next two centuries.

27
Liu Xiu
The empire reborn

The winter night was cold as 300 people in civilian garb trudged along a moonless road. Their uneven steps broke the silence with the crackling of dry leaves underfoot.

Their leader Liu Xiu received messages from his scouts. A four-hour march behind them, 50,000 imperial soldiers were on the hunt and ready to take them prisoners. But blocking the path less than 20 miles ahead of Liu and his 300 men was a wide river, frigid but not frozen.

Liu had to take a gamble. Would the night grow cold enough to freeze the flowing rapids? Or would they be cornered and cut to pieces on the dark shores?

Then two scouts returned, but only to confirm the leader's fears. In whispers, they told Liu Xiu that the air was still warm and the river dangerous.

Liu held back his worries as he looked from face to face of his thin, battle-weary, wild-eyed men. If they stopped or retreated now, they would be crushed. The only way out was forward.

"The river has frozen!" Liu Xiu announced! The commander left their fate to the heavens, and the 300 hastened their march.

The heavens answered. Within an hour, temperatures began to fall and a strong northern wind prevailed. The river flowed slower and was soon frozen solid in a layer so thick that not just men, but beasts and carts could drive across. The 300 laid branches on the ice and wrapped their horseshoes in cloth to avoid them from slipping. Then they hurried across the expanse.

No sooner had they crossed, the wind stopped and the air warmed. By the time the imperial army arrived at the bank, all they saw was the mighty river and their prey on the other shore, already escaping far into the distance.

It was the year AD 23. The Roman Empire was advancing further north into Europe. Augustus would soon avenge the shock and humiliation German tribal hero Hermann inflicted upon the Roman legions a decade earlier in Teutoburg forest.

In China, the mighty Han Dynasty was going through an unprecedented crisis. In the year AD 9, Chancellor Wang Mang seized power, wielding the imperial seal as first (and only) emperor of the Xin or "new" Dynasty. Sixteen years later, the people revolted against his idealistic but disastrous rule.

Without strong authority though, the rebels had no leader and began to fight amongst one another. The better-organized imperial army could simply take them on group by group and crush them like hordes, as they almost did as mentioned the beginning of this chapter.

Liu Xiu, the rebel commander who was saved by the

weather, is also called Emperor Guangwu of Han. He was a ninth-generation descendant of Liu Bang, who founded the Han Dynasty. But nearly 200 years had passed, and Liu Xiu's family enjoyed only a small imperial pension as a reminder of their noble heritage. Liu's father was a mere county magistrate.

Because the family's simple abode was hot and humid, Liu Xiu's father moved his pregnant wife to the nearby palace of Emperor Wu. It had not been in use for 80 years and would serve as a better delivery room, at least. According to legend, a red glow illuminated the entire palace as she gave birth to a chubby baby boy. In another sign of coming fortune, the harvest that year bore grains with nine ears.

Liu's father followed these good signs and named the baby "Xiu," which describes the blooming and ripening of crops.

Liu Xiu was gentle and prudent—quite the opposite of his restless elder brother Liu Yan. Liu Yan was proud of his muscular warrior's physique and would laugh at his brother's meekness. Meanwhile Liu Xiu busied himself with the harvest, toiling in the fields and herding cattle. Still, he made a point to devour books.

The brothers' father died when Liu Xiu was 9. To make matters worse, Wang Mang's destruction of the Han Dynasty meant that the Lius could no longer collect their imperial pension. To make some pocket money, Liu Xiu bought some donkeys and did work as a porter for passing by travelers. He was generous and gave some of what he made to his less-well-off friends.

Yet when it came to fight, Liu Xiu was no mere peasant. In the year 22, people were taking up arms against Wang Mang's misrule and Liu's brother Yan was among them. The other

Lius were skeptical, but when they saw that the educated and soft-spoken Liu Xiu stood with his older brother, they too joined in.

The image of a fearless Liu Xiu waving a heavy machete on his ox was a constant inspiration to his peers, and later earned him the name "bull-riding emperor."

Brave and determined were the Liu brothers' legions, and in no time their followers grew tenfold. Many generals fighting for Wang Mang admired them so much that they welcomed them with open city gates.

But the Lius' generals, who disliked following strict discipline and were only given limited power, prevented the royals from taking their rightful place on the imperial throne.

Instead, the generals chose as their leader another imperial descendant, the weak-spirited Liu Xuan. He was easy to control and was even fine with the generals letting their men steal from civilians. Liu Xuan infamously asked his puppet-masters: "How much loot did you guys get today?"

Liu Yan and Liu Xiu's wartime accomplishments became their curse. The jealous Liu Xuan, now called Emperor Gengshi, set up a meeting with Liu Yan, who was appointed prime minister. But it was actually a trap and Liu Yan was murdered in cold blood.

Liu Xiu was still fighting on the front lines when he received the news. The general's subordinates were seething with anger and the envoy shook in their boots. One word from Liu Xiu could have the envoy put to death and a powerful army marching back to oust the Gengshi emperor.

Rather than letting himself be overtaken by rage and

hatred, Liu Xiu gritted his teeth and held fast to the sword. Revenge would only bring chaos. In order to fulfill his vow and restore peace to the country, he would have to put his personal feelings aside.

Finally, in late 23, Liu Xiu defeated the main enemy force in the Battle of Kunyang. Wang Mang was killed and the Xin Dynasty was no more.

Unlike the similarly short-lived Qin Dynasty, which unified China's territory, language, and culture, Wang Mang's 16-year-reign had few positive contributions.

Liu Xiu returned to the capital while maintaining his calm. He never boasted about his military achievements or bemoaned the injustice done to his brother. Ashamed, Emperor Gengshi decided to give him a promotion.

Another reprieve that came at an otherwise dark time in Liu's life was marrying Yin Lihua, a sweet and caring beauty who lived in his hometown. With nothing to offer but his romantic sentiments, a young Liu Xiu sighed: "If I were to marry someone, it would be Yin Lihua."

No longer short of money and accomplishments, Liu Xiu's childhood dream came true.

Lihua was a descendant of Guan Zhong, the legendary minister of the state of Qi over 500 years earlier. With almond-shaped eyes, eyebrows curved like willow leaves, and two rose-tinged dimples that deepened with the movement of her delicate cherry lips, Yin Lihua's beauty was the pride of her parents.

But Lihua's greatest asset was her humble and virtuous personality. When Liu Xiu became emperor, she gave up her position as empress to her rival in the imperial court who was chosen for political reasons. But Liu Xiu never abandoned her and she eventually became empress after many years.

Liu Xiu bided his time, and eventually it came. Unsurprisingly, neither Emperor Gengshi nor the generals who controlled troubled by effective or popular leaders, and China was still filled with rebel armies and large gangs even a year after Wang Mang's death.

One particularly large and fearsome secret society was the Chimei, or Red Eyebrows. They attacked the imperial capital and ousted Emperor Gengshi, replacing him with a fake emperor.

Liu Xiu, who was already busy fighting the new rebels, simply moved his army into the capital and restored order. He became Emperor Guangwu in AD 25. The name means "bright and martial," an apt description of his reign.

28

Zhang Daoling
The Heavenly Master

The respectable Lady Chen in a rural village suddenly went crazy. Chen's family was typical among Chinese peasants, consisting of her parents-in-law, siblings, as well as her three young kids. A humble, caring, and unselfish woman, Chen played a key role in resolving conflicts within the huge family. The onset of her ailment shocked everyone.

One day, an eccentric person came to the village. He wore a long beard and shabby clothes, but it was hard to tell his age, as he had a youthful, glowing complexion.

The man went straight to Chen's door and asked for food. As he finished eating, he said: "There's an evil demon hiding in your house. Someone must have been ill for a while. I may be able to help."

When Chen saw the man, a disturbed and angry look appeared on her face. She began jumping about, mumbling some sounds that no one could understand. Moreover, she looked afraid. The old man pointed to Chen, saying aloud: "In the name of Lao Zi, I banish thee!"

He took out a gourd with one hand, reached out the other, grabbed at something in the air, and rammed it into the gourd.

Chen immediately calmed down. She opened her eyes, and her expression returned to normal.

The old man said: "Lady Chen was possessed by a spirit. I have contained it in the gourd, so you don't need to concern

yourself about it anymore." Chen was very weak. Before he left, the old man wrote out a prescription, and told Chen's family to prepare the medicine for her.

This old man was Zhang Daoling, a student of the Old Master Lao Zi. Because of his superior personality, he was also called Zhang Tianshi, or "heavenly master."

Lao Zi taught the Tao or Way, but Zhang Daoling created the Taoist religion.

Before the Han Dynasty, China did not have a religious system. Taoist cultivators, whom the Chinese often referred to as hermits or Taoist practitioners, usually kept to themselves and were not concerned with society at large. Even Lao Zi wrote a book of just 5,000 words before leaving his job to live in seclusion.

Born around 40 BC, Zhang Daoling was very bright and was able to read at an early age. However, he was not interested in common knowledge, but devoted himself to the philosophy of Lao Zi. When he was around the age of 40, Zhang Daoling left home, travelling south in search of a Taoist master. It is said that he had several masters who taught him many cultivation methods. He then reached entry-level enlightenment on Mount Longhu.

Zhang later perfected his practices in the hills of northern Sichuan Province. He cultivated both internal and external alchemy. But unlike earlier Taoists, he also frequently travelled about in society, helped treat illnesses and taught people to improve their character. Gradually, a large number of people came to follow him.

Zhang refused money from his followers or the patients he healed. Instead, he collected five "pecks" (about 25 kg) of grain from each person, which he stocked in a barn to assist the poor.

While in Sichuan, it is said that Zhang met Lao Zi, who had enlightened to the heavenly Tao, and learned his advanced practices. After completing cultivation, Zhang was venerated as "heavenly master," and the Taoist movement that he founded became known as Five-Pecks-of-Grain Tao or Tao of the Heavenly Master (Tianshi Tao). Zhang revered

Lao Zi as "Taishang Laojun," which literally means the Grand Supreme Old Lord. His book of 5,000 words was named Tao De Jing.

The Heavenly Master asked his believers to treat heaven, earth and living beings with respect, and live a life according to the principles of the four seasons and the natural way. When coming across issues such as illness, one should first reflect on himself or herself in a quiet room and write down the thoughts on paper. One should then burn the paper while praying to heaven and show resolution to correct the mistake. Zhang Daoling also imparted Taoist techniques to disciples, so that they could handle evil spirits.

The external alchemy method in Tianshi Tao produces supplementary medicine through various organic and inorganic substances, which eventually developed into China's earliest study in chemistry. The most famous invention was the creation of gunpowder, a by-product of this alchemy.

In Tianshi Tao, disciples were free to marry, drink, and eat meat, as long as they followed a plain and simple lifestyle, conformed to the laws of nature and stayed away from worldly affairs. Tianshi Tao did discourage eating four kinds of animals for the virtues they embodied. The first was the grey mullet, a kind of fish that searches for food to feed its parents even when they are little, representing the Chinese virtue of filial piety. The second was the cow, an important work animal in agricultural production that is contented with eating grass, which represents industry and simplicity. The third was the swan goose. This bird stays with only one mate throughout its lifetime, symbolizing respect for marriage. The fourth was the dog, which possesses a loyalty hard to find even in humans.

Many true Taoists follow these rules even today.

It is said that Zhang lived over 120 years before finally

obtaining the Tao in Mount Qingcheng of Sichuan.

Zhang Lu, Zhang Daoling's grandson, later succeeded to become the third leader of Tianshi Tao. During the Three Kingdoms Period when China was in chaos, the locals elected Zhang Lu as their political and military leader, maintaining public order and business operations in the region. Zhang Lu avoided fighting other warlords whenever possible. When Cao Cao (pronounced "tsao tsao"), King of the state of Wei, attacked Zhang Lu's territory, the Taoist leader, who was not attached to any political power, simply retreated his forces.

Unlike other military leaders, Zhang Lu refused to burn grain and supplies—the "scorched earth" tactic often used to prevent enemy armies from living off the land they conquer. Zhang said,

"This is the people's blood and sweat. We can't sacrifice the well-being of the masses for the sake of our power." He sealed the storehouses and assigned guards to protect them.

Zhang Lu then sent Cao Cao detailed lists recording the contents of the storehouses. Touched by Zhang Lu's act of benevolence, Cao Cao offered a peace deal, promising to put aside past conflicts and not to levy additional taxes on the region. Zhang Lu accepted it. He surrendered his troops and returned to ordinary life.

Tianshi Tao remains an important branch in the Chinese Taoist religion, being passed on through direct descendants of the Zhang family. In 1949, Zhang Enpu, the 63rd Tianshi, moved with the Nationalist Party to Taiwan when Mainland China was conquered by the communist army. His nephew Zhang Yuanxian inherited his title, becoming the 64th Tianshi.

29
Lü Bu
The End of a Tyrant

The year of 184 was a harsh one for China. Suffering corrupt government, foreign invasion, and droughts for years, the peasants reached their boiling point. Tying yellow scarves to their foreheads and calling themselves the Yellow Turbans, they launched a massive rebellion, delivering the Han Dynasty a severe blow. For the next ten years, generals and warlords rose to power and fought with the rebels and each other to restore order to the land.

Two ruthless and ambitious conquerors, the twisted prime minister Dong Zhuo and military officer Cao Cao, stepped into prominence.

In the imperial court of the failing Han Dynasty, prime minister Dong Zhuo craved absolute power and had the means to seize it. The fiercest soldiers from foreign lands served him, as did the imperial army in the capital. The Han emperor was just a child, and he was under the protection of his mother. Dong Zhuo murdered the empress, then slew the emperor easily. He placed another young boy on the throne, but made it known to that he was the one with the real authority, Dong arrogantly carried a sword to the imperial court and openly mocked the puppet ruler.

Dong Zhuo even owned a castle with walls as high as those of the capital Chang'an itself and demanded that all visitors and passersby dismount their horses and pay respects. He named the castle "Imperial Walls"—a reference to the vast power he held in his hands.

The ruthless Dong not only killed to get into power, he also killed people for pleasure. Like Roman emperor Nero, Dong Zhuo had captured rebels wrapped in oil-soaked cloth, hung upside down, and set them on fire.

Dong had hundreds of captives dragged in front of him and his men during a feast. As the wicked prime minister and his subordinates dined, the prisoners' tongues were cut off, their eyes gouged out, and four limbs hacked off.

And just in case anyone tried to harm Dong Zhuo, there was the seven-foot-tall Lü Bu to reckon with.

The fearsome "flying general," as Lü was known, was such an exceptional warrior that whoever had him on his side was undefeatable in combat. This super soldier was Dong's adopted son, so the tyrant felt he had nothing to fear.

The common people loathed Dong Zhuo so much that they circulated songs wishing for his death. At the same

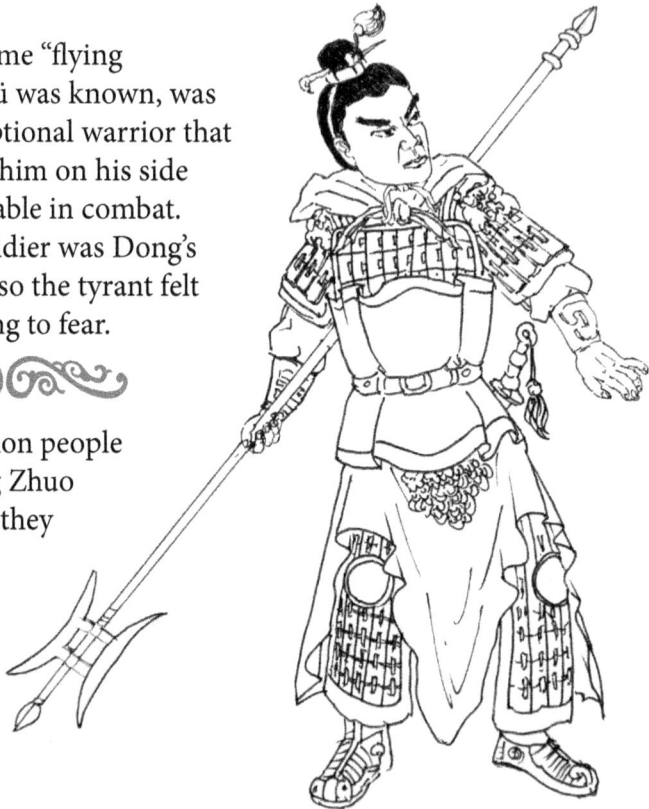

time, his rule was so brutal that almost nobody in the government dared lift a finger against him. The exception was Minister Wang Yun.

Wang was determined to rid the country of the tyrant, but he knew that he was not powerful enough to do it directly. Instead, he did his best to comply with Dong Zhuo's wishes. Wang soon won his trust and took over court affairs while secretly looking for a way to kill him.

Meanwhile, a man named Cao Cao was burning with the same passion. Though still a military officer of low rank, Cao Cao had made a name for himself fighting the rebels, and was a valued guest at Dong Zhuo's palace. Like Wang, he too was waiting for an opportunity to slay Dong.

Wang Yun met Cao Cao at a birthday party and was impressed by the young soldier's aspirations. To carry out the mission, Wang gifted his renowned Seven Star Sword to Cao Cao, who took it to Dong's palace.

Cao Cao successfully convinced Dong Zhuo to send the fearsome Lü Bu away on an errand, but unfortunately, the attempt failed when Dong noticed Cao Cao unsheathing his sword. Cao Cao barely escaped with his life by claiming that the prized weapon was just a gift. Dong Zhuo, who was in a good mood, forgave him.

Cao Cao fled immediately as fast as his horse would take him, and Dong Zhuo understood what had happened. He stepped up security measures in the palace and, ordering Lü Bu to follow him everywhere. Wang Yun had to find a different, more cunning method.

Wang paced about his courtyard, where blooming flowers sweetened the air. His worries lessened for a moment as he took in the scene. Then his adopted daughter appeared, her smooth face gleaming in the moonlight.

This was Diao Chan, one of the Four Beauties of ancient China. At a young age, she had become an orphan and grew up by Wang Yun's side. By the time she was 18, she was already well-known for her beauty. It was said that her face was so radiant that it put the moon itself to shame.

Diao Chan was indebted to Wang Yun, who had taken her in and raised her. She was constantly looking for ways to return the favor, and seeing the anxiety on his face made her feelings even stronger.

And as Wang Yun looked at the girl he had raised as his own daughter, he found the key to killing Dong Zhuo.

⁓⁓⁓⁓

The following day, Wang Yun invited Lü Bu to his mansion. As the men feasted, Diao Chan entertained them with song and dance. Her light ivory gown flowed with the movements of her alluring form, drawing everyone's gaze.

Lü Bu was invincible in combat, but Diao Chan conquered him easily. He was all too delighted when Wang Yun offered to make them man and wife.

Wang's simple, cold-hearted, but absolutely effective plan had begun. A few days later, Lü Bu was devastated to see Diao Chan in Dong Zhuo's palace.

Lü Bu went to Wang and called him a liar. What was his love doing with his adopted father? For the first time, he felt anger, jealousy, and revulsion towards the tyrant that so many others hated.

Wang was used to playing the right act. Wearing an innocent look, he expressed utter sadness and regret. Dong Zhuo, he said, had met Diao Chan earlier and wanted to add her to his collection of girls. Dong Zhuo being who he was, Wang Yun had no way to refuse.

The love triangle involving Lü Bu, Diao Chan, and Dong Zhuo destroyed the relationship between the two men. When spending time with Dong Zhuo, Diao Chan would pull at his heartstrings by telling him how Lü Bu was giving her unwanted attention. And when she snuck out to meet Lü Bu, she wept and sobbed about her fate of being forced to be with Dong Zhuo, an overweight man who was more than old enough to be her father.

A desperate Lü Bu went to Wang Yun for advice. Wang told him that Diao Chan was already engaged to him, so Dong Zhuo was in the wrong even if he was Lü Bu's adopted father and the prime minister.

It did not take long for the lust-possessed Dong Zhuo to catch Lü Bu and Diao Chan in his courtyard. In a mad rage, the ruler drew his sword and went after the warrior. It was no contest. Lü Bu's battlefield instincts kicked in as he confronted his enemy. The old and obese Dong Zhuo died immediately.

All rejoiced at the death of the once-formidable despot. Lü Bu reunited with his sweetheart, as commoners celebrated with firecrackers throughout the capital. Dong's fat body was thrown on the street. Soldiers ignited candles on his navel. There was enough fuel to burn for days.

Dong Zhuo's death did not bring an end to the chaotic situation. One month later, his old subordinates attacked Chang'an and killed Wang Yun. Lü Bu sought refuge with several warlords. Eventually, he was betrayed by his men and tied up while he was asleep, then brought before Cao Cao. Lü Bu offered to serve him, but Cao Cao deemed him too dangerous and had him put to death.

It is not known what happened to Diao Chan, or even if she was a real person. But her story is passed down through many famous literary works, and historical documents do suggest that Lü Bu killed Dong Zhuo in the year 192 over a love-fueled disagreement.

Cao Cao later became the leader of the Wei Empire, controlling all of north China. It was one of three states—the others being Shu and Wu—that emerged after Dong Zhuo's death. Thus began the era that is the setting for the great Chinese novel, "Romance of the Three Kingdoms."

30

Cao Cao
The mightiest warlord

*H*aving tried and failed to kill Dong Zhuo, military officer Cao Cao fled the tyrannical prime minister's estate as fast as his horse would take him.

Cao Cao was now a wanted man, but it did not take him long to find friends. As people heard how he had attempted to take Dong Zhuo's life, he became a hero overnight. With the help of a wealthy merchant, Cao Cao established his own army and prepared for war.

This failed assassin would become the powerful warlord of Wei, one of the Three Kingdoms.

In AD 192, Dong Zhuo was killed by his adopted son Lü Bu. Without their leader, Dong's frightened henchmen launched an open rebellion against the Han emperor. The emperor fled his palace and looked for help, only to find that his entire government had abandoned him.

Seeing his chance, Cao Cao marched with his men to the capital and pledged his loyalty to the Han Dynasty. He took the terrified emperor under his wing as China exploded into warfare all around them. The imperial palace was burned to the ground and rebel armies were everywhere. Cao Cao's support was critical, and he soon became the most powerful man in the Han court.

Cao Cao's greatest enemy was his former comrade Yuan Shao. The numbers were bleak: Yuan had amassed over

700,000 men against a Han imperial force just a tenth that size.

But Cao Cao knew Yuan Shao well and was confident that he could win. The enemy commander was a short-sighted man who was blinded by his quest for power, Cao Cao reassured those around him. Yuan Shao's ten-to-one advantage would simply fuel his arrogance and recklessness. For Cao Cao, there were plenty of opportunities to seize victory.

Cao Cao chose Guandu, a port near the Yellow River, as the best place to establish his base. As Yuan Shao's troops pursued them, the Han soldiers intentionally scattered jewels and other treasures on their path of retreat. As expected, Yuan Shao's men laughed at their enemies. But as time dragged on, they became distracted by the shining gems and gold. They even began to bicker about the treasures and drew weapons on each other.

When Han scouts reported this to Cao Cao, he knew the moment to attack had arrived. Though outnumbered, his men entered their battle formations and charged, catching their enemy completely off-guard. Yuan Shao lost one of his best commanders in the first battle, and Cao Cao moved his men to Guandu.

Still, Yuan Shao pressed on. Soon, Guandu was surrounded and under siege. With 20,000 men, Cao Cao held the enemy at bay for months, but supplies were running low. It seemed like everything they did was only delaying their doom.

To cheer up his desperate and hungry soldiers, Cao Cao promised them that he would defeat Yuan Shao in just 15 days. In fact, the Han forces could barely hold for another month. It would again be Yuan Shao's arrogance that turned Cao Cao's bold declaration into reality.

One night, Cao Cao received an unexpected guest. It was his old friend Xu You, who was serving under Yuan Shao as a top strategist. Xu had followed Yuan Shao when he rebelled against Dong Zhuo, but lately sensed that Yuan no longer listened to his advice. In fact, the general even claimed that Xu You was corrupt. As a distinguished scholar with a high reputation, Xu could not tolerate this insult and fled to Cao's camp.

Xu You told Cao Cao about Yuan Shao's greatest weakness: the storehouse in Wuchao. This base was about 40 li away from Yuan's headquarters and contained supplies for nearly his entire 100,000-man force. Without it, the army would collapse.

Cao Cao immediately put together a squad of 5,000 men. They disguised themselves as Yuan Shao's troops and marched off at nighttime. Slipping through the lax enemy defenses, Cao Cao personally led his warriors into the camp and started a massive fire that consumed all the precious grain stored at Wuchao. Then Cao Cao launched an attack on his enemy.

As Xu You had predicted, Yuan Shao's troops crumbled. They were used to a string of easy victories and discipline took second seat. As chaos spread, Yuan Shao's troops either surrendered or ran away.

Yuan Shao escaped with just 800 men. He never recovered from the defeat and died a year later, in 202.

Yuan Shao's army left behind much treasure during their flight. Cao Cao gave all of it to his men and kept none for himself. Along with the jewels and riches were letters of conspiracy between his trusted aides and Yuan Shao. Cao Cao could have easily killed these traitors by checking the names and handwriting, but he refused, displaying neither anger nor shock.

"Facing the powerful Yuan Shao, let alone others, even I was struggling merely to preserve my life."

He calmly burned the letters. His subordinates sighed in relief. In their hearts, they felt even more loyal to their leader.

But Cao Cao also had his distrusting side. Xu You, the man who had helped Cao Cao defeat Yuan Shao, did not live long. He spoke too often about his role in the victory, and also publicized some embarrassing episodes from Cao Cao's youth. Xu had a fight with another officer, and was killed. Some historians believe this quarrel was set up by Cao Cao to get rid of him.

Cao Cao did not keep his promise to serve Han loyally. Instead, he disposed of the emperor and declared himself the founder of a new dynasty, Wei. This was one of the famous Three Kingdoms, along with Shu and Wu.

In his quest to unify China, Cao Cao was eager to attract gifted men to serve him regardless of their origin. One example was how he treated Guan Yu, the sworn brother of Liu Bei, who founded Shu. The red-faced and full-bearded Guan Yu was Liu Bei's bravest warrior and fiercely loyal.

Cao Cao and Guan Yu met when Guan Yu was surrounded by Wei soldiers. Guan Yu was defending the area where Liu Bei's wife and son were hiding, so he knew the only way to save their lives would be to surrender.

Though it was clear that Guan was committed to Liu Bei, Cao Cao did not treat him like a captive. Instead, Guan Yu was given the treatment of a general, and allowed to travel around the camp as he pleased. He was given good food and many gifts.

But Guan Yu only expressed gratitude when Cao Cao presented him with a rare steed, the legendary Red Hare that could gallop 1,000 li in a day. "With its help, I can meet Liu Bei within a day of learning his whereabouts," Guan Yu said.

After being given the horse, Guan Yu acted on his words. He escaped to Liu Bei in Hebei, taking with him only his horse and sword. But Guan Yu did not forget to show gratitude to his captor. Before escaping, he managed to kill a general in Yuan Shao's army.

Their next encounter was to be eight years later, at the famous Battle of the Red Cliff.

The years leading up to AD 208 passed with blessings for Cao Cao. He officially became the prime minister of Han, the same position that Dong Zhuo had enjoyed. Wei's territory dramatically expanded with the defeat of various northern warlords. Aside from most of the areas north of the Yangtze River, Cao Cao also obtained an elite army consisting of 20,000 fierce nomadic warriors. His only two remaining rivals were Liu Bei and Sun Quan, but the forces of even the two of them put together were of no match for Cao Cao. Cao Cao was 54, still in his prime, and his vision of a China united under his rule was within grasp.

That July, Cao Cao decided that it was time to march south. He gathered up his 200,000 soldiers—four times of the number of Liu Bei and Sun Quan's men combined—and prepared to cross the Yangtze River. To further scare his enemies, he claimed the number was 800,000.

Cao Cao was so confident of his forthcoming victory that

he set up a feast while crossing the Yangtze River to celebrate. The round moon gleamed at him from the night sky and from the flickering water. Cao Cao gulped down a cup of wine and wrote:

> *The moon outshines the sparse stars; the crows fly to the south*
> *circling the tree three times; on what branch can they find rest?*
> *Mountains do not despise height; Seas do not despise depth.*
> *The sage pauses when guests call, so at his feet the empire does fall!*

Cao Cao imagined that he was a reincarnation of the revered Duke of Zhou, who oversaw the golden age of China's longest-lasting dynasty. Perhaps he should have thought of Yuan Shao, whose arrogance had led him to ruin.

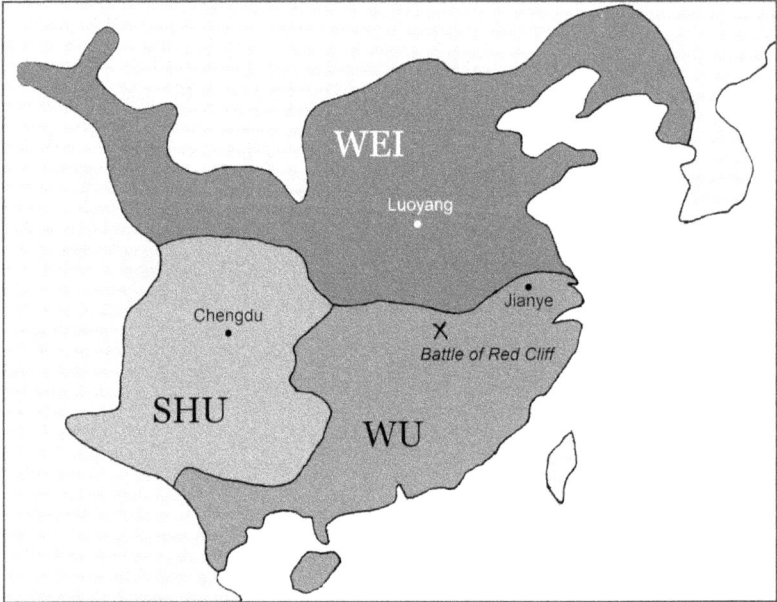

China's famous Three Kingdoms Period lasted 60 years from the fall of the Han Dynasty in 220 to 280 AD, the beginning of the Jin Dynasty.

31
Liu Bei
Heroes of the Three Kingdoms

Twenty-four years before Cao Cao set off with his army to cross the Yangtze River, three young men met in the city of Zhuozhou. Gathered in a garden of blossoming peach trees, they burned incense and said prayers.

Each one carried three sticks of incense. They all knelt and made vows to heaven, promising that from that point on, they were all brothers and would serve each other and the country for the rest of their lives.

"Much as we were not born on the same day, in the same month of the same year," they said in unison, "we ask that we die together, on the same day in the same month of the same year."

Of the three men, the oldest was the 28-year-old Liu Bei. The others were Guan Yu and Zhang Fei, two huge and powerful fighters.

This is the beginning of the most famous tale of brotherhood in Chinese history. The Han Dynasty was coming to an end. China was entering the famous Three Kingdoms era.

Liu Bei, Guan Yu, and Zhang Fei sold all of their property and organized a few hundred men to prepare for war. They joined the government army and fought very well. Liu Bei was a wise and righteous man, and a distant relative of the first Han emperor, Liu Bang. Zhang Fei and Guan Yu were powerful warriors and almost unstoppable in combat.

At first they joined the warlord Cao Cao, whom we introduced in the last chapter. But as time went on, it became clear that Cao Cao was not loyal to the Han, as Liu Bei wished. Instead, he kept the Han emperor under his control, making himself and his family the real power behind the throne.

Now it was the year 208. If Cao Cao won the Battle of Red Cliff that was unfolding on the Yangtze River, he would have mastery over all of China.

In addition to the forces of Liu Bei and Cao Cao, a third power silently arose in the years of chaos. This was the government and army of Sun Quan, a man who some say had ancestors in the Caucasus Mountains between Europe and the Middle East. According to historical records, he had pale skin and blue eyes, and his hair was blond or brown. However, his official family tree says that his ancestors came from the Yellow River region.

The Yangtze River area was not as developed and not as culturally rich as the Yellow River, where Chinese civilization had sprouted. It was easy for Sun Quan to set up his government and gain support.

When Cao Cao came charging towards the Yangtze River with a massive army of 200,000 men, Liu Bei and his two sworn brothers were hiding on the northern riverbank under the protection of a local general. The general saw the strength of Cao Cao's army and decided to surrender. Liu Bei was firmly against the idea, and decided to retreat to the south. After a series of daring battles, he gathered around 10,000 men and found a riverside city in the middle reaches of the Yangtze, where he planned his last stand.

This was when Sun Quan came in and lent his assistance. Still they only had about 60,000 men put together—they were outnumbered about one to four.

But history has some wild cards, and numbers alone do not win wars. Many small rivers sprang from the Yangtze itself, making it difficult for Cao Cao's troops to move. They were used to fighting on open plains and did not have enough boats to navigate the waters properly, let alone fight well. So instead of going to battle immediately, Cao Cao had his troops conduct drills.

Sun ordered a large number of special unmanned boats filled with oil and other flammable material to be sent drifting towards the enemy. But there was one problem: it was winter and the prevailing winds blew south, not east as was needed. Still, the forces of Sun Quan and Liu Bei had no other hope.

What happened on the day of the operation was nothing other than fate: the wind did something it never did in winter before, and began to blow east, straight towards Cao Cao's fleet. Sun Quan sent out his burning ships, causing a tremendous fire to break out among Cao Cao's forces. In confusion, Liu Bei's and Sun Quan's troops launched an attack by land.

Before Red Cliff, Cao Cao had been almost certain that he would win easily. But the attack against Cao Cao's 200,000-man army was so devastating that he escaped from the Yangtze with only a small number of his men.

After his victory, Liu Bei took his army west and conquered the region of Shu, now China's Sichuan Province. With his ally Sun Quan, who ruled the land of Wu, and Cao Cao's empire of Wei, Liu Bei became an important leader in China's famous Three Kingdoms Period.

There are many dramatic stories from the adventures of Liu Bei and his comrades Guan Yu and Zhang Fei. Sometimes they suffered defeat and were separated, at other times, they were tempted to betray each other. But ultimately, the three men stayed loyal to their sworn brothers and uphold the principle of justice they had vowed to defend when they took their oaths in that orchard of peach blossoms.

Because Liu Bei was honest and cordial, he attracted many illustrious helpers. One of them was the young but brilliant genius Zhuge Liang. After several personal trips to his home, Liu Bei, Guan Yu, and Zhang Fei finally persuaded him to join Liu's army.

In the year 220, Cao Cao died and was succeeded by his son. Cao's son decided to get rid of the Han emperor altogether so that he himself could become emperor of a new dynasty, the Wei.

Hearing the news, Liu Bei decided it was up to him to keep the Han Dynasty alive, so he too declared himself emperor.

Sun Quan followed suit, calling his dynasty the Wu.

Decades passed as the three empires fought to control all of China. Usually two sides would team up to take on the third side, only to betray each other after a while. Typically it was Liu Bei's inherited Han Dynasty and Sun Quan's Wu that found a common enemy in the powerful Wei.

In one battle between Wu and the Han, Liu Bei's loyal warrior Guan Yu was killed. Zhang Fei too died, this time at the hands of an assassin who escaped to Wu.

Greatly angered, Liu Bei ignored the advice of his adviser Zhuge Liang and mobilized all his troops to attack the forces of Sun Quan. But he failed, and died soon afterward.

The stalemate continued, until Cao Cao's descendants were thrown out of power by the Sima family, just as they had done to the Han. In 265, China was unified under the Jin Dynasty.

1,400 years later, a man called Luo Guanzhong read the historical annals and wrote a famous novel, the Romance of the Three Kingdoms. In over a hundred chapters, he crafted a moving and vivid drama that is popular all across East Asia today. Even though much of it is fiction, the Romance of the Three Kingdoms influenced many Chinese and spread to Korea, Japan, and other countries. The first emperor of China's last dynasty, Nurhaci of the Qing, used the book as his guide to war and diplomacy.

32

Zhuge Liang
The Crouching Dragon

It was the winter of 208. Half a million soldiers stood ready on the northern bank of Yangtze River. Their armor blanketed the landscape in dark metal.

Across the river, 60,000 troops belonging to a different army braced for the coming battle. The northern army was ready to win. Not only did they outnumber the foe nearly ten to one; but their hundreds of large, agile vessels could also travel easily through the river and strike wherever they pleased. Victory seemed certain.

Early in the morning, heavy fog enveloped the area. Except for a tiny streak of light on the distant horizon, darkness reigned. The sentries of the northern army were on high alert. They kept their eyes peeled and an ear to the ground.

From a watchhouse came an emergency report: an unknown but large number of southern vessels were approaching. A drumbeat started and grew steadily louder. Attack seemed moments away.

As the river condition and the enemy's motives were unclear, northern commander and warlord of the Wei empire, Cao Cao, was put on the defensive. Tens of thousands of archers went into action.

Arrows rained down on the enemy ships. The fleet seemed perturbed, and loitered about for some time before leaving as the fog dispersed with the rising sun.

The southern troops cheered as the ships sailed back to

shore. These ships belonged to warlord Sun Quan, king-to-be of the Wu Kingdom. Scarecrows fastened to them were the "soldiers" Cao Cao and his men saw through the fog. The fleet brought back over ten thousand arrows, replenishing Wu's dangerously low supply.

The person to credit here was Zhuge Liang, a renowned military strategist in the Three Kingdom era.

Zhuge Liang was just 28 and led a peasant lifestyle, yet already he was recognized as the sagacious strategist of the time. He was nicknamed "the Crouching Dragon" for the lifestyle he had had before making his appearance in the battle along the Yangtze.

A year earlier, Zhuge was still living in Nanyang, shielded from the chaos in the world at large. When Liu Bei, king of Shu, came by, he was delighted to learn about this young genius and was eager to meet him in person.

Twice Liu Bei went to consult the Crouching Dragon and twice he was greeted with an empty house. The third time, determined to see Zhuge, Liu Bei got up very early and went again, accompanied by his two sworn brothers Zhang Fei and Guan Yu. The trio found Zhuge Liang sound asleep. Unaccustomed to such a reception, the two brothers were only too impatient to leave. But Liu Bei stopped them, and the three waited in the courtyard.

The mysterious Crouching Dragon showed up at last—surprisingly young considering his fame. Point by point he analyzed the balance of power in the Central Plains, and concluded that the lack of a solid territorial base was Liu Bei's greatest weakness. He would need a strong base if he wanted a powerful army.

Cao Cao in the north and Sun Quan in the east were Liu's major rivals. Both had established their governments; only the mid-upper reaches of the Yangtze River lay unclaimed and lawless. He advised Liu Bei to take over the large western province of Sichuan, then called Shu, and ally with Sun Quan to contend with the powerful Wei under Cao Cao's control.

Everything suddenly fell into place. As a descendant of the Han royal family, unifying China and restoring the glory of the Han Dynasty was Liu's dream. Zhuge Liang showed him the way. Greatly impressed, Liu Bei asked Zhuge to join him in his campaign. Zhuge soon rose to become Liu's most trusted aide.

Shortly after, Cao Cao, the most powerful warlord of the three, attacked Liu Bei. With less than twenty thousand soldiers, a fraction of Cao's troops, Liu Bei's only option was to retreat. He fled southward all the way to the Yangtze River. With Zhuge's aid, Liu made alliance with Sun Quan. That was when Zhuge helped Sun Quan borrow arrows.

Next came the Battle of Red Cliff, where Zhuge Liang lent legendary assistance in defeating Cao Cao.

As described in the previous chapter, Liu Bei and Sun Quan planned to attack Cao Cao's fleet with fire. It was winter and the prevailing northerly wind blew in their direction, making it difficult if not impossible to carry out a fire attack on Cao Cao's forces without immolating their own troops.

Zhuge Liang again came to rescue. He volunteered to "negotiate" with heaven to borrow the eastern wind. As he busied himself with the construction of an altar, he ordered

Sun Quan's troops to prepare for the attack. For seven days he prayed. On the very day of the attack, the wind miraculously changed course, and Cao Cao's fleet was destroyed. The kingdoms of Shu and Wu were saved.

Zhuge Liang was not only a military and political expert, but he was also gifted in astronomy and geography. The story of "borrowing arrows" as previously depicted was a masterful display of his expertise. Cao Cao's troops came from the north and were unfamiliar with the southern terrain. They would exercise caution by refraining from advancing in bad weather, and would only shoot in defence.

Soon, Zhuge Liang helped Liu Bei occupy Sichuan Province, the upstream stretch of the Yangtze River. In two years they also took a large part of the southwestern land. Sichuan was a vast stretch of fertile plain protected by mountains. Liu Bei finally gained a stronghold in China—the Shu Kingdom.

The southwestern ethnic groups near Sichuan would not bend so easily. They constantly caused trouble to the Shu Kingdom. Zhuge did not seek to conquer by force. He captured the rebel leader seven times. Yet when the life of the troublemaker was in his hand, Zhuge set him free. The rebel chief was so moved that he vowed fealty to the Shu Kingdom forever. He became Zhuge's chief assistant in the south.

When Liu Bei was old and near death, he was worried that his son was not fit to be emperor. He told Zhuge Liang, "My son is still young, I haven't observed any wisdom or virtue in him that sets him apart, so I will give you complete authority. If you think he is worthy, then by all means help him; but if not, you can take his place."

Zhuge was moved to tears. "I was a mere young farmer unknown to the world. You discovered me and gave me a chance to realize my ambition. I will strive to restore the power and prestige of the Han Dynasty, and assist your son until I die."

He kept his words. Although Zhuge had absolute control over the army and court, he never abused his power for his own interests. Throughout his life, he kept battling with the Wei Kingdom of Cao Cao and struggled to revive Han, as Liu had wished.

Despite all the power and prestige, Zhuge had little to give to his sons. His legacy consisted of a humble abode, five acres of land, and a dozen fruit trees. Zhuge's most famous line—"I give my all to what I am doing until the day I die"—has become a metaphor for loyalty and dedication.

Integrity, intelligence, and a little mystery made Zhuge Liang one of China's most beloved historical figures. People revered him so much that they constructed a memorial hall in Shu's capital Chengdu, where it still stands today.

33
Sima Yi
The end of an era

*T*he sage strategist Zhuge Liang is well known as the definitive genius of the Three Kingdoms Era. In terms of wit, capacity, and intellect, none was his match, except for Sima Yi, the man who would bring an end to the era.

Sima Yi served as a top advisor for Cao Cao, emperor of the Wei Kingdom. His acute insights and prudence earned him the leader's trust eventually, no small feat considering Cao's tendency to suspect others.

"Serving the king is tantamount to living with a tiger," ancient Chinese warned. Sima Yi showed that this did not have to be the case, and enjoyed a smooth political career despite being the top general and at one time the prime minister. But no matter how high his position

was, Sima always kept a low profile, giving everybody the impression that he was an assiduous worker whose only desire was to do a good job and nothing else.

Towards the end of the Three Kingdoms Era, many of the battles between Wei and Shu resembled state-sized games of chess between master strategists Sima Yi and Zhuge Liang.

Facing the powerful enemy, Sima avoided direct confrontation. The long, steep hills surrounding Wei served as a natural shield. Zhuge Liang was often forced to retreat when their supplies ran out.

Sima had another reason for adopting a defensive strategy. Generals who fought with Zhuge Liang invariably suffered setbacks, but Sima could preserve Wei without losing anything himself. By keeping the Wei border secure, he was also establishing his credibility. He knew that enemies were also his asset: he made sure not to completely eliminate the outside threats, so as to remind Emperor Cao Cao that he depended on him.

In AD 234, Sima's long-time rival Zhuge Liang fell ill in a military expedition and died shortly thereafter. Though they had been enemies, Sima Yi felt like he had lost a companion of sorts. He wept for a long time.

Sima's family enjoyed considerable influence in Wei. His nine sons were all distinguished officials. Sima served four Wei emperors, each less capable than the previous one. The fourth emperor, Cao Fang, was only eight when he ascended the throne, and the imperial court fell into the hands of the child's uncles. They saw Sima Yi as a threat to their power.

Just like the strategy he adopted in dealing with Zhuge Liang, Sima Yi also avoided direct confrontation with the Cao family. He complained about his failing eyesight and claimed that he was ready to retire. It was understandable—he was already in his 70's.

Sima did not enjoy much peace after he withdrew from court affairs. The emperor's uncles kept a watchful eye on him, constantly sending people to inquire about his condition. Sima Yi knew that he was in danger, so he feigned illness. Whenever someone came visiting, his hands would tremble so violently that medicine would spill from his bowl. He mumbled incomprehensible words and let saliva flow down his collar and sleeves.

Believing Sima Yi to be near death, the imperial uncles loosened their guard.

In AD 249, the emperor went to the outskirts of the capital to offer sacrifice, as did his uncles. The entire capital was left to Sima Yi himself. With help from his sons and his allies in court, he immediately assumed control of the army. In the name of rooting out "crooked chancellors," he had those who suspected him killed. The Sima family took over the Wei Kingdom and ruled from behind the scenes with the real emperor as a figurehead.

Sixteen years later, Sima Yi's grandson Sima Yan did away with the story that the Cao family was still in power. He made himself emperor and created the Jin Dynasty. By this time, the kingdoms of Shu and Wu were quite weak, and they fell in AD 280. The Three Kingdoms Era was over.

34
Hua Tuo
A doctor before his time

In the year 220, the fierce warrior Guan Yu was shot in the arm by a poisoned arrow. His comrades were all worried.

That day, a doctor arrived. He told Guan Yu: "I could purge the poison, but I wonder if you can bear the pain." Guan Yu said, "I have been a soldier for years. I'm not scared of pain."

The doctor said, "Okay, put your left arm through this iron

ring. Then have the rest of your body, including your right arm, tied to this wooden stake." Guan Yu was confused. Why did he have to be tied up?

"The poison has gotten to your bones," the doctor said. "I need to open up the wound and shave off the infected parts."

Upon hearing this, Guan Yu called over a staff officer and began to play Go with him. He told the doctor that he could begin the operation. By the time the doctor was done, Guan Yu had lost enough blood to fill a couple of large bowls. The staff officer was terrified as he heard the sounds of bone being filed off, and the soldier who was holding the bowls to catch the blood screwed up his eyes. Only Guan Yu sat there, almost totally unfazed.

The surgeon exclaimed, "General Guan Yu, you're really no ordinary man."

This story is not just about the bravery of the warrior Guan Yu. It is also one of the first recorded instances of Chinese surgery. The surgeon's name was Hua Tuo, and he was one of China's most renowned doctors.

Hua Tuo could understand the causes and cures of various kinds of illnesses. By looking at his patients' facial appearance and complexion, he could tell what kind of problems they were suffering from. He could even tell if they would live or die. Many of his observations are similar to those used in modern medicine.

For instance, most people could not take the kind of pain that Guan Yu could, so Hua Tuo invented a herbal broth that served as an anesthetic. This allowed him to perform surgical operations on patients who would otherwise be impossible to bear the pain.

Inventing this drug was partly a matter of skill and partly of chance.

Hua Tuo once had a patient who had fallen unconscious. He lay still on the ground, his jaw locked and his eyes wide open. Hua Tuo checked his pulse and body temperature, but everything seemed fine. The man was previously well-built and healthy. His family reported that he had simply consumed a few flowers of a plant called the "foul devil's snares."

That was Hua Tuo's first contact with the plant. As the name suggested, it emitted a foul smell. He chewed a petal, and immediately his mouth became numb. Recognizing its effects, Hua Tuo thought he could use it to do good. Coincidentally, the flowers happened to grow near his in-law's house. Hua Tuo gathered a bundle of them for experiments.

The doctor's concern for his patients overcame his fear for his own safety. He tasted every part of the plant—leaves, flowers, fruits and roots. After much trial and error, and having tried out numerous different herbs, he finally found the proportion that could make patients unconscious without endangering them. Prepared with warm wine, the potion was so powerful that the patient would pass out before the operation and not feel any physical pain. That was the first appearance of anesthetics in China, and possibly in the world. Common folk held Hua Tuo in such awe that they thought he was a living immortal who possessed the magical powers of gods.

It's not known for certain where Hua Tuo learned his medical skills from. His fame comes from the many folk tales and stories about his deeds.

At seven, Hua Tuo lost his father. His mother also died of

illness when he was 12. The pain that his mother suffered before her death motivated him to become a doctor to relieve people of physical torture. He headed west and found a medical guru in Qionglin Temple, and asked to become his student.

Hua Tuo's first task was to take care of patients. He boiled water, served tea, cleaned chamber pots and bandages, all with incredible patience, and paid meticulous attention to detail. He observed patients' condition and appetite, and took note of the medicines they took.

Three years later, Hua Tuo was well versed in different illnesses and their treatments. His teacher decided he was worthy of further instruction, so Hua Tuo spent the next three years devouring the books at Qionglin.

The ultimate test came one day when his teacher was ill. The guru's face had turned waxy yellow and saliva dripped from the corner of his mouth.

Hua Tuo was the only one to stay calm among the

panicking students. After some observation, he said: "Don't worry, our teacher is fine."

His indifference would have caused an uproar had it not been for the sudden voice of the teacher: "Correct. I pretended to be ill to see how well you have learned."

When Hua Tuo returned to the study, he was shocked to find a pile of ashes where his books had once been. The candle flame had burnt the books. Immense guilt immediately overcame him. He had just accidentally ruined his teacher's most treasured possessions, he thought.

Luckily, he had studied them thoroughly and his memory was fresh, so he decided to write everything down as well as he could. It took him a month to finish. Just as he was putting the pages together, his teacher walked in and smiled.

It turned out to be the final test for Hua Tuo. His teacher had hidden the books to see if he had the courage to face the wrong and make up for it. The fact that he could reproduce the materials from scratch also showed that he had learned them by heart. His training was complete.

Hua Tuo did not let his teacher down. He could often relieve patients of pain by inserting a few acupuncture needles into them. Because of the chores he did as an apprentice, he also became so familiar with herbs that he did not have to weigh them when filling prescriptions but simply grabbed the exact amount he needed. He was careful to identify the root cause of illnesses and prescribe the cure accordingly.

On one occasion, two patients came to him for fever and headache. Hua Tuo decided that the first one, Ni Xun, needed to take laxative; to Li Yan, he prescribed a drug to help him sweat. The two were baffled about the differing treatment. Hua Tuo explained: "Ni Xun suffered an internal injury which harmed his spleen but Li Yan came down with a cold. The treatments therefore differ."

Hua Tuo also used psychotherapy. There was a governor who suffered from an unknown illness. After examining him, Hua Tuo told his son, "Your father's case is peculiar. There's a lot of blood congested in his stomach. He has to spit it all out to recover."

Hua Tuo knew that medication would not work on him, so he adopted the unconventional method and asked the son to cooperate with him.

Hua Tuo purposefully demanded a large sum of reward but did not do any work. After a few days, he quit abruptly. Soon, the governor received a letter from him. The letter was full of cynical and condescending criticism that jabbed at every one of the governor's shortcomings. The governor was infuriated. He wanted Hua Tuo captured and killed immediately. As he flew into a rage, he vomited a large amount of dark blood clots and was cured of the disease.

Hua Tuo's fame spread all over China. He was particularly active in the territory of Wei, which was ruled by Cao Cao. The latter was plagued by constant headaches, and sent for Hua Tuo.

Hua Tuo applied acupuncture whenever Cao Cao's head ached, and the pain would go away. He also cured Cao Cao's young son. Cao Cao was so impressed that he wanted to make Hua Tuo his personal doctor.

But if Hua Tuo became a court doctor, he would not be able to serve anyone but Cao Cao and his family. Countless ordinary people would not be able to receive treatment from him. He excused himself by saying that he needed to stay home to care for his ailing wife.

Hua Tuo also revealed that the root cause of Cao Cao's headaches was cancer and that the only way to cure him was to open up his skull and take out the tumor.

Instead of letting Hua Tuo operate on him, Cao Cao threw him in jail, thinking that the doctor was after his life. At the same time, he did not want his skills to be used anywhere else. "If I can't use him, he can't serve anyone else either."

Shortly thereafter, Hua Tuo died in the terrible conditions of the dungeon.

As Hua Tuo predicted, Cao Cao's illness got worse. He remembered the doctor and looked for him, but it was too late. Not only did Cao Cao die of cancer, but his son, the most brilliant of his children, had died at a young age, soon after Hua Tuo perished in captivity.

Cao Cao's family was eventually removed from power by Sima Yi.

35
Sima Zhong
China plunges into chaos

*T*he young man sitting on the imperial throne in Luoyang was confused when he received a messenger who had hurried in from the northern province of Hebei. The land was experiencing drought and the people were starving because their crops would not grow. But the emperor's response revealed that he was totally out of touch with his subjects.

"Why don't they eat meat instead?" he asked the messenger in disbelief.

This was Sima Zhong, emperor of the Jin Dynasty. Though he was just the second emperor, his dynasty would soon be over.

To call Sima Zhong a dimwitted man would be putting it politely, considering the kind of things that occupied his mind. One evening, he strolled about in his garden, wondering aloud to his ministers: "Are the frogs croaking for the sake of the kingdom or for a personal reason?" The officials did not know how to reply without insulting their ruler's intelligence, so they kept quiet.

Historical record suggests that Sima Zhong lacked the common sense of even an average man, not to mention capability to manage an empire.

It was especially strange considering that Sima Zhong's father, grandfather, and forefathers were exceptionally brilliant men who ended the Three Kingdoms Era and united China just a few years earlier.

His father, Sima Yan, never wanted Zhong to be emperor for long. He chose him as his successor because he adored his grandson, Sima Yu, who was Zhong's son and was very clever.

On one occasion, when Yu was six, a fire broke out in the palace. Sima Yan ascended a tower to try to find out what was happening, but his grandson tugged at his sleeve, saying: "Your Majesty should not stand near the fire. We don't even know who or what caused the fire. What if someone is planning a conspiracy against you? It's dangerous to stand here in such a conspicuous place."

Sima Yan was impressed that Yu was able to consider all this at such a young age. And when the emperor had Sima Zhong's fortune told, he was pleased to hear that the dimwit was not fated to live long. Getting Sima Yu on the throne of Jin was now a possibility.

Sima Yan died in the year 290. Sima Zhong was incompetent as expected, but the woman he married, Jia Nanfeng, was a crafty and intelligent empress. Unfortunately, she was also wicked and selfish. Sima Yu was not her son, so she had him removed from the position of crown prince. Her jealousy led her even further to have him poisoned at the age of 22.

Empress Jia used all her smarts to stir up conflicts between the many members of the Sima clan. Sima Yi, grandfather of the Jin Dynasty's first emperor, had nine sons, Sima Yan had 18. Members of the Sima family who did not become emperor were given power in other areas, especially the military, and Jia Nanfeng did not trust them.

But eventually the empress's plots got the better of her. In the year 300, a Sima prince led an army to Luoyang and killed Jia Nanfeng. A civil war broke out among eight princes and their armies, called the "War of the Eight Princes." Each claimed they were on a "peacekeeping" mission to protect the emperor. This went on for seven years until one of the princes decided things would be better with himself on the throne instead, so he sent a general to kill Sima Zhong.

In his final moments, Sima Zhong showed that even a fool can have compassion. When the enemy general came for his head, he pleaded with him: "Kill me if you like, but please spare my bodyguard!" The general ignored him and killed the guard, whose blood splattered over the emperor's clothes. As Sima Zhong was led away to be executed, he refused to remove his dirty robes out of respect to his bodyguard.

The death of Sima Zhong was a disaster for the Jin Dynasty. The next emperor was seen as illegitimate and the country was thrown into even greater chaos. A general of the Xiongnu people (he was actually Chinese from a cultural perspective) led his army to Luoyang and slaughtered the Jin Dynasty imperial family.

Ever since Emperor Wu of Han conquered the nomadic peoples living on China's borders, many of them had moved deeper into China. Some took up Chinese culture, but others continued their old tribal way of life.

Unlike the native Chinese, who busied themselves with farming, these tribal minority groups kept their warrior tradition. They took advantage of the chaos under the Jin Dynasty and rose to power. Soon, armies of nomadic people were marching and riding across all of North China.

The tribal peoples envied the wealth and refinement of Chinese culture and civilization. Many Chinese fell victim to the nomads, who killed indiscriminately and pillaged the riches of civilization along the Yellow River. This disaster became known as the *wu hu luan hua*, or the Revolt of the Five Barbarian Tribes.

Between the years 300 and 380, five million people migrated from the north to the south, a sizeable chunk of the total Chinese population at the time. Many of them were wealthy families, noblemen, and scholars—people who would not accept being ruled by barbarians and had the money to migrate. The survivors of the Jin Dynasty imperial family fled to Jiankang (modern day Nanjing), where they established the Eastern Jin.

Thus, after less than two generations since the Three Kingdoms Era, China was broken up again. For the next 200 years, northern China was under the control of nomadic tribes. The south, particularly the regions around the Yangtze River, were under traditional Chinese control and maintained many aspects of the old society.

The five tribes, including the Xiongnu, built around 16

different states in northern China around the Yellow River. Five dynasties appeared briefly in southern China. Historians call this 200-year schism the "Northern and Southern Dynasties."

This time period was filled with warfare and social change. Around 50 years after the death of Sima Zhong, a nomad prince called Fu Jian temporarily united the north and established the Former Qin Dynasty. He built up an army of nearly 1 million men and marched south to take on the Eastern Jin.

36
Fu Jian
The battle that split China

Military flags blotted out the sun and war drums thundered along the waters of the Fei that ran between the mighty Yellow and Yangtze rivers. Over 800,000 foot soldiers and horsemen were marching south, ready to annihilate the 80,000 defenders that had rushed out of Jiankang to take the enemy on.

Fu Jian, emperor of the Former Qin, commanded the northern armies personally. His victory was assured, or so he thought.

It was the year 383. A century earlier, China had been temporarily united under the Jin Dynasty after decades of civil war that brought down the mighty Han. Then, nomadic tribes took over northern China while establishing their own empires. By the mid-4th century, the empire called Former Qin united the entire territory of China north of the Yangtze River, while remnants of the Jin, China's sixth dynasty, held out to the south.

Emperor Fu Jian was anxious to make all of China his, and facing the pitiful eastern Jin forces, wanted to do battle immediately.

But among all of Fu Jian's ministers, generals, favorite palace ladies, and family members, few thought this to be a wise plan. The troops of the Former Qin were strong and numerous, to be sure, but they hailed from different barbaric states and were difficult to control. Their allegiance was connected to the military rations they received from their generals, not loyalty to the empire. And after long periods of civil war, they longed for peace.

Suspiciously, the only people in Fu Jian's court who supported the war were from other tribal groups. They had other intentions, but Fu Jian, confident in his numbers, did not see this and believed their words.

When the people and officials of the Eastern Jin heard of the massive army heading their way, the capital city of Jiankang was taken by panic. Yet Prime Minister Xie An remained calm, as was his style. He was not much of a strategist, yet he would help lead his country out of the predicament.

Xie An ordered his brothers Xie Xuan and Xie Shi to take command of the Jin army and meet the oncoming Former Qin troops.

Meanwhile, Fu Jian sent Jin general Zhu Xu he had captured to deliver a message to his enemies, asking them to surrender or face a bloody battle.

Zhu Xu met with Xie Shi, but instead of ordering him to surrender, revealed critical information: most of the Former Qin soldiers were still on their way to the battlefield. Seizing the opportunity, the Jin army sent out a 5,000-strong elite combat force to attack the Former Qin soldiers already at the scene, killing 15,000 enemy troops.

Fu Jian and his top general Fu Rong were surprised and wondered if the enemy they faced was actually as small as they had previously imagined. Still, Fu Jian decided to press on. "My army is so enormous that if all the men throw their whips into the water, the river's flow will be broken."

Then the Jin generals used an expert stratagem: they sent a messenger to Fu Jian, offering to take their forces over to the western side of the River Fei in exchange for a retreat of 5 km for the Former Qin troops. Then the two armies would fight honorably.

Fu Jian was delighted. Basic tactical sense told him he would be able to attack the Jin army as it crossed the river and destroy it easily. Some of his generals warned him, but he and Fu Rong ignored them. The Former Qin army began to retreat.

In an era without telecommunications, it is difficult to deploy hundreds of thousands of men even without the chaos of war. To make matters worse, Fu Jian's army consisted of soldiers from various tribes and speaking many different languages. They already loathed attacking; the order to retreat simply confused them further.

Meanwhile, the captured Jin general Zhu Xu had come back to the Former Qin. Walking about behind the front lines, he sounded a false alarm: "The Qin army has been defeated! The Qin army has been defeated!"

Now it was the northerners' turn to panic. The massive army began to fall back and become paralyzed with fear, as one unit after another passed on the "news." Men, chariots, and horses jammed and trampled on one another trying to escape. Supplies and weapons were abandoned in masses.

The Eastern Jin troops launched a full-scale attack. They triumphed easily as their proclaimed victory became reality.

When the message of victory arrived Jiankang, Prime Minister Xie An was playing Go with his friend in his mansion. He opened the letter, read it, and put it down as if nothing had happened. His companion was overcome with

anticipation and asked Xie An what the outcome of the battle was. "Nothing much. Our boys seem to have won."

Most of Former Qin's troops starved, ran away, or were
killed in the retreat. General Fu Rong died in action. Fu
Jian had no way to recover from his loss. Across northern
China, other tribal leaders began to challenge his power. This

included those who had encouraged Fu Jian to launch his attack on Eastern Jin in the first place, since it was their plot to weaken the power of Former Qin.

In 385, Fu Jian was killed by his own men. The north fell apart completely as the Xianbei, Xiongnu, Rouran, and other tribes established territorial boundaries and governments. The Eastern Jin empire in southern China continued on for some time before giving way to other dynasties in AD 420.

While China was at war and suffered disunity for hundreds of years until the Sui Dynasty came to power in 581, many changes occurred that shaped the national culture, language, religion, and even racial characteristics. The northern barbarians became used to living in the same land as the Han people and using Han characters (Chinese writing). They named their dynasties in Chinese and intermarried with the Han ethnic group. Many of them became indistinguishable from Han Chinese.

At the same time, from India and the West came monks who learned Chinese and translated the scriptures of Buddhism. In 500 BC, Buddha Shakyamuni had cultivated to the level of Tathagata and taught his disciples the Theravada way of Buddhism. Buddhism, which teaches the universal salvation of sentient beings, became an important part of Chinese culture and traditional faith. It is considered one of the traditional Chinese religions, the others being Taoism and Confucianism.

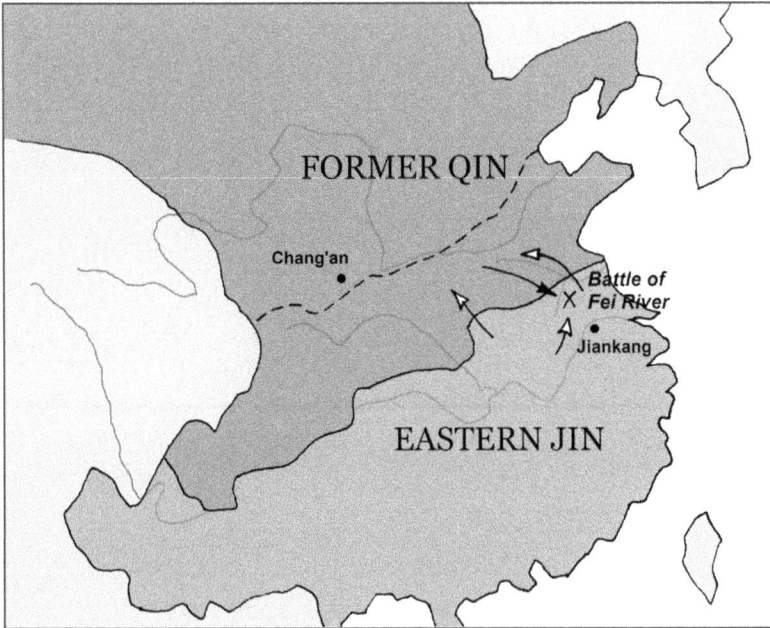

In AD 383, the Eastern Jin Dynasty defeated a massive 800,000-man army at the battle of the River Fei. China remained divided between the Northern and Southern Dynasties for 200 years.

Timeline of Events

CHINA	TIMELINES	WORLD
	c. 4000 BC	Beginning of Sumerian civilization
	c. 3100 BC	Beginning of Egyptian civilization
Reign of the Yellow Emperor	2798 BC	
	c. 2600 BC	Emergence of Mayan and Indian civilizations
	c. 2200 BC	End of the Old Kingdom in Egypt
Yu controls the Great Flood **Xia Dynasty** *(1st Dynasty)*	c. 2000 BC	
	1895 BC	Beginning of the Babylonian Empire
Shang Dynasty *(2nd Dynasty)*	1600 BC	
	1200 BC	The Trojan War
Zhou Dynasty *(3rd Dynasty)*	1046 BC	
	800 BC	Rise of the Greek states
Spring and Autumn Period	770 BC	
	660 BC	Founding of Japanese imperial line
	563 BC	Birth of the Buddha
Birth of Confucius	551 BC	

CHINA	TIMELINES	WORLD
	539 BC	Fall of Babylon
	508–509 BC	Beginning of Athenian democracy and Roman Republic
	480 BC	300 Spartans defend Greece against Persia
Warring States Period	475 BC	
	470 BC	Birth of Socrates
	331 BC	Alexander the Great conquers Persia
Qin defeats Zhao in Battle of Changping	260 BC	
Qin Dynasty unifies China *(4th Dynasty)*	221 BC	
Han Dynasty *(5th Dynasty)*	206 BC	
Invention of paper	200 BC	
	146 BC	Rome defeats Carthage in the Punic Wars
Reign of Emperor Wu	141 BC	
	44 BC	Murder of Julius Caesar
Defeat of the Xiongnu nomads	36 BC	

CHINA	TIMELINES	WORLD
	27 BC	Founding of the Roman Empire
	AD 1	Birth of Jesus Christ
Liu Xiu reunifies China after fall of Wang Mang	36	
	79	Volcanic eruption at Pompei
Buddhism spreads to China	100s	
The Three Kingdoms Era	220	
Jin Dynasty *(6th Dynasty)*	280	
	285	Rome splits into eastern and western empires
Five Barbarian tribes take over north China	304	
	313	Roman emperor Constantine I legalizes Christianity
Battle of the Fei River	383	
Fall of the Jin Dynasty	420	
	441	Attila the Hun tries to conquer Roman France
	476	Fall of the Western Roman Empire

CPSIA information can be obtained
at www.ICGtesting.com
Printed in the USA
LVHW112322131218
600433LV00001B/66/P